Whenever I went ashore, I was enchanted by the beauty and variety of a prospect which was terminated by the noblest forest in the whole world. . . . .

From Father Charlevoix's Journal
1682 - 1761

SUMMER RESORT LIFE:
Tango Teas and All!

Revised Edition

Published by Jet'iquette
Charlevoix, Michigan
49720

Printed by Canfield & Tack, Inc.
Rochester, NY

Dear Reader:

It is with a great deal of pleasure and pride that we have funded the printing of this revised history of the community. Our bank and its predecessors, Charlevoix County State Bank and First State Bank of Charlevoix, have been a part of Charlevoix for over 110 years. We are proud of our community and its history.

We are pleased to respond to the many requests for a re-print of <u>SUMMER RESORT LIFE: Tango Teas and All</u>, and to a general need for a comprehensive history of the development of our lovely community.

We hope that you will treasure this book and enjoy it for years to come.

Sincerely,

Francis B. Flanders
Chairman, President and CEO

ABOUT THE AUTHORS:

EDITH GILBERT is the author of *The Complete Wedding Planner, All About Parties, Let's Set the Table.* She is currently working on her next book. She is a syndicated and feature writer for major newspapers. She has summered in Charlevoix since 1940 and has lived here year round since 1962.

PAT McKEOWN, JR. has his degree in Business Administration and a master's degree from Michigan State University. He is married to Wendy and lives in Charlevoix. He is the comptroller at Pat McKeown Ford Inc., and has a lively interest in the history of the area.

The late BERNICE CRANDELL WEXSTAFF was the author of several children's books, all based on the historical background of the area. She was a member of the DAR and lived in Charlevoix her whole life.

DEE ANN ROTHENBERGER was born in Charlevoix and is a retired schoolteacher. Her article "Pine River and Bridges" is an excerpt from a paper prepared for Studies of Michigan History, Central Michigan University, 1970, from where she received her master's degree.

TABLE OF CONTENTS

REVISION:

In this revised edition of *SUMMER RESORT LIFE: Tango Teas and All!* we have not altered the original text.

The reader will consequently please notice that a number of persons referred to on the following page have since passed away, and we beg your indulgence.

ACKNOWLEDGEMENTS:

We are deeply grateful to all those people who gave so freely of their time, but especially to the late Earl Young, who was extremely kind in sharing information, clippings and brochures. We are also indebted to the generosity of Robert Miles for both his personal recollections and his wonderful photographs.

We greatly appreciate the co-operation of the librarians, Mary Beth Wallick and Eleanor Ratigan of the Charlevoix Public Library, and a special "thank you" to Bob Clock and Ken Winter for giving us access to the film strips of the Charlevoix Courier.

Also, we wish to thank Charlevoix's County Clerk, Grover Geneit, for his willing cooperation in searching through old records and files in his office. The laborious job of proofreading was carefully done by Bonnie Staffel.

In addition, we are obliged to the countless Charlevoix citizens who patiently submitted to our questions during private interviews and who frequently jogged our memory. They are as follows:
Marian Bridge, Lila Bedford, Elizabeth Clark, Chas. Carey II, Jeanette Cameron, Peg Driggett, Beverly Eby, Kay Fitch, Slim Gerhart, Julius Gilbert, Ralph Hamilton, Richard Lowenstein, Don Meggison, Mr. & Mrs. Richard Moss, Dan McSaube, Jay Oliver, Marion Purdy, Mildred Paddock, Dr. & Mrs. Gilbert Saltonstall, Freda Stewart, Mr. & Mrs. Edward Shanahan, Vane Smith, Mark Smith, Dr. Jules Stein, Jack Uhrick, Mr. & Mrs. D.D. Walker, and Laura Jean Wulfman.

INTRODUCTION:

Now comes the moment when one gathers up all the papers, photographs, notes, etc., and drops them in the printer's lap with the hope that every instruction will be followed, every scribbled note deciphered correctly. For months people have been questioned, prodded not only in person, but over the phone and by mail. Facts have been checked and double checked. Words counted, decisions weighed and now at long last, there it is — laid bare for everyone to read, to weigh and yes, even dispute.

The materials selected for this commemorative booklet cover the first half century, but mostly the turbulent period between World War I and World War II, when places like Charlevoix reached their peak as family summer resorts.

We hope this glimpse into the recent past will help future historians portray more factually the varied life styles during this colorful era of the flapper girl, Prohibition and the Great Depression, as well as the years shortly before and after.

The results, we hope, will lift the veil of memory for many "old-timers" and pique the curiosity of the young. But better yet, we pray these little vignettes will narrow the distance between generations, for whenever we glance back, we can't help but notice, with a chuckle, the similarities between then and now as well as the differences.

It must be remembered that during any adversity — such as wars and economic upheavel — the well-to-do families, instead of travelling abroad, retreated to a "summer cottage." Consequently, it follows that during "hard times" the resort communities throughout the United States prospered.

The Railroad Station, for example, was a sparkling reflection of resort life. The bland scenes at airports today can't compare with the excitement of going to the depot, just for the fun of it! say on a Sunday evening in July or August to say "goodbye" to people who were leaving. Here was a lively picture, indeed. Tanned travellers dressed in business suits ready for work on Monday morning; young men carrying golf bags, tennis racquets and fishing poles; children very carefully placing pennies on the track; uniformed maids holding dogs on leashes; chauffeurs pushing wheel chairs; cooks and nurses leaning on steamer trunks and guarding assorted plants, Petoskey stones and pieces of driftwood picked up on the beach that afternoon — everyone's eye turned north, waiting for the first glimpse of the train, the first puff of smoke, the first whistle.

It is true we've written not only about one specific town — Charlevoix, but we've compounded this rashness by concentrating on one specific street, Michigan Avenue, which is only 4 blocks long if you count the last block leading to the Pine River Channel. Yet the development is so typical of all resort towns not only in Northern Michigan, but just about anywhere in America during this period, we feel justified in taking this approach. Wherever the railroad built hotels, resorters followed. They built their clubs, their golf course, their yacht docks, their tennis courts. They enforced their blue-laws and winked at the swank gambling casinos nearby. They sometimes drank liquor from tea cups and danced the tango to live bands. Towns that welcomed resorters prospered while neighboring farm villages frowned with genuine disfavor at "these goings on." Without a doubt, the influence of the "summer people" in the resort communities on the young "natives" was enormous. A teenager caddying on the golf course, was asked by a resorter, "What college are you going to son?" when the idea of attending ANY college had never before entered his mind! Needless to say, he went to college and is now a high school principal.

On the other hand, the home-spun influence of the "natives" on the "summer people" has been equally felt. The trend today is for the simpler life, and more and more resorters winterize their "cottages" into year-round homes. Houses that were boarded up in the winter are now brightly lit twelve months out of the year, because "the season" — thanks to winter sports — has no beginning and no end. The distinguishing traits between a resorter and a native walking down the street today have become blurred.

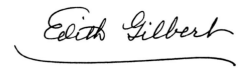

4

In conclusion, there are some who may complain at the lack of good photographs presented in this booklet, but good photos are hard to come by. Our own family albums, and we have many, are typical of what is around: numerous pictures of fish and lakes, children and pets, dim groups of nameless faces posed in front of a tree or bush, usually of an undated time and unrecorded place. Forgive us this lack, we hope to call attention to this need of identifying family photographs and in some cases turning these over to your local historical society.

Edith Gilbert

HISTORICAL HIGHLIGHTS:

Anyone genuinely interested in the history of this area will profit by a nostalgic visit to the Michigan Room in the Charlevoix Public Library. Here one will find a substantial collection of books on sailing, fishing, lumber and the railroad industry, as well as an outstanding photography collection graciously donated by Robert Miles.

1721   Voyage of Father Charlevoix, a Jesuit priest, from Detroit to Michimilimackinac.

1837   Michigan became a state.

1850   James Jesse Strang, a Mormon, was crowned King of Beaver Island.

1853   So-called "Battle of Pine River," a scrimmage between Mormon settlers from Beaver Island and the Charlevoix "Gentile" fishermen.

1854   First permanent settlers arrived in Charlevoix.

1861   First log schoolhouse built on banks of Round Lake.

1867   First grist mill erected on Pine River and first sawmill put into operation on site of present Charlevoix Lumber Co.

1869   Charlevoix County organized and village of Charlevoix became county seat. Charlevoix *Sentinel* printed the first issue of its paper. The widening and deepening of Pine River Channel was begun.

1873   Grand Rapids & Indiana Railroad passenger train arrived in Petoskey. The first church (Methodist) in Charlevoix was under construction.

1875   Indians were deeded many acres of land by the U.S. Government along the shores of Lake Michigan.

Summer resorters followed the railroads and the subsequent associations were usually organized according to religious denominations, such as Methodists, or by groups of friends from such cities as Kalamazoo.

1876   Bay View Resort[1] was founded by Methodists.

1878   Harbor Point Association founded by Episcopalians from Lansing, Michigan.

Wequetonsing Association founded by Presbyterians.

The Belvedere Club founded by Baptist ministers and teachers from Kalamazoo, Michigan.

1880   The Chicago Club was founded by leading members of the First Congregational Church in Chicago.

1902   Sequenota Club[2] was founded by a group from Galesburg, Illinois, home of Knox College.

1881   Lewis Grand Opera House was built.

1882   The first steel swinging bridge across Pine River was officially opened.

1892   The first train arrived in Charlevoix.

1896   The *S. S. Manitou* made its first trip through the channel into Round Lake.

1 Dudleigh Vernor, organist for 62 years, wrote "Sweetheart of Sigma Chi."

2 *Seventy Years of Sequanota History.* 1930 Directors' meeting. It was "moved, seconded, carried — that the girls be allowed to have a VICTROLA in the Reception Room of the Club House."

1898 The INN HOTEL, built by the Chicago & Western Michigan Railroad, was completed.

1899 The original BEACH HOTEL was under construction.

1920 The COLONIAL CLUB (Koch's) opened.

1938 The first commercial airplane service started to Traverse City. (An airfield in Pellston was cleared in 1939.)

1945 The Charlevoix Airport was put into operation.

1947 The COLONIAL CLUB was closed.

1962 The U.S. Coast Guard Station moved from Lake Michigan to its former buoy yard on Round Lake. The Department of Natural Resources now occupies the former station.

1971 Archeological dig by Michigan State University began on the site of the former Beach Hotel, now La Croft Condominiums.

1975 Promenade walk on north side of Pine River Channel completed.

1982 Last train left Charlevoix.

1984 Railroad Bridge was removed.

1994 Bellinger Marina torn down.

What's New
In Charlevoix

by
Edith Gilbert
(*Detroit Free Press*, May 6, 1973)

Not much, if anything, has been written about Charlevoix during that golden period beginning after World War I and climaxed with the Great Depression — when the pre-jet set flocked north during July and August from sizzling Chicago, humid Detroit, torrid St. Louis, and sweltering New Orleans, their monogrammed steamer trunks loaded with ermine wraps for the ladies to wear on cool Michigan evenings and for the men, white silk tuxedos and black patent leather dancing shoes.

> "On the high hills on the north bank of Pine River where the ancient Indian Factories for making arrow heads were once located . . . the skies of Italy are not more genial; France is not more fruitful; Venice presents no more beautiful waterscape than does Charlevoix."

> *Charlevoix Courier*, 1918

This was the period when Charlevoix was known as the queen of northern Michigan summer resorts and the popular Beach Hotel, overlooking Lake Michigan, was one of its crown jewels. Here, on the north bank of Pine River, summer visitors gently rocked on freshly painted white porches and smugly played the game of one-upmanship.

"I've been coming here for twelve summers!"

"Consecutively ?"

Fifth generation summer people who still play "I've been here longer than you have" sometimes forget that before THEY discovered the place, there were prior visitors: bearded Mormon settlers, ruddy Irish fishermen, hardy Finnish lumberjacks, adventurous French fur-traders, scholarly Jesuit explorers, and, of course, the very earliest inhabitants, friendly Chippewa Indians.

Thousands of well-to-do city folk came north during the 20's to spend their air-cooled summers at the resort hotels. They played tennis and golf in the morning and, thanks to prohibition, they danced to tango teas in the afternoons. They gambled at tony casinos at night.

According to the *Charlevoix Courier*, 1921, the young "flappers" made front page news:

"Charlevoix has stepped into the limelight as a 'bathing suit' town. There are girls here who don their bathing suits when they doff their nighties and wear them all day. Some have gotten so brown, except for the smaller portions of their shapely anatomies that do not show, that they resemble the members of the tribe that once owned the site of Charlevoix and there's nothing scandalous about it, no indeed! Policemen don't chase them like those rude Chicago policemen would, because the Charlevoix policemen think they look nice and isn't Charlevoix a place where they come to relax? And doesn't Charlevoix want the pretty mermaids to come back next season?"

Charlevoix is a bathing suit town. "There are girls here who don their bathing suits when they doff their nighties and wear them all day."

Of course they do! The next season and the next, with their mothers, fathers, sisters, brothers, cousins, and aunts because this was and still is a family resort. The same people who toss hundred dollar chips on the roulette table at night are seen toasting marshmallows on the beach and viewing steropticon pictures or exchanging gossip in the fumed oak tea room the next day.

"Dora is still in mourning. She left her rubies and sapphires in Chicago this season — and only brought her diamonds !"

But mostly mothers plot meetings between their marriageable sons and daughters. Marriages may be made in heaven, still this generation didn't take any chances! Every season, family relationships and family fortunes were consolidated. Scores of couples, still married, first snuggled together on the dance floor in the ballroom of the Beach Hotel — while parents lined one and two deep along the ballroom walls.

The seven-story Beach Hotel and cottages on Lake Michigan showing Round Lake and Lake Charlevoix beyond.

Photo taken from the air by Robert Miles, 1954

Downstairs ballroom decorated for a private party during the 40's for Mr. and Mrs. Henri Meis, Danville, Illinois.

Photo by Robert Miles

And let's not jump to the erroneous conclusion that the dances then were all that tame. One Baptist minister turned thumbs down on the "turkey trot caper and buttermilk slides, hurdy-gurdy twists and wiggletail glides" as inspired by the devil himself ! He writes:

> "Backward, turn backward, Oh time in your flight,
> Give us a girl with skirts not so tight;
> Give us a girl, no matter what age,
> Who won't use the streets for a vaudeville stage;
> Give us a girl not too shapely in view;
> Dress her in skirts that sun can't shine through."[1]

The Beach Hotel held its formal opening in 1899 and the first season "could not be well termed a success as the 'hotel' contained about 15 rooms and one bath, there being no office, a desk in the corner of the dining room being utilized for this purpose. In 1904 the building was enlarged, the roof raised and housing capacity practically doubled. Since this period each year has increased the popularity of the Beach." [2]

The hotel prospered under the capable management of its owner, Martha Baker,[3] and in 1915 she commissioned Clarence Hatzfeld, a prominent Chicago architect, to design "a new haven of splendor." Built entirely of wood, the building rose 7 stories high on the lake side and grew to 216 rooms with 86 baths. An ornately grilled elevator was installed in the lobby and a dining room was included that seated 400 guests — which is bigger than any dining room in the area today!

---

1 *Charlevoix Courier,* June 24, 1914.

2 *Charlevoix Courier,* Jan. 18, 1922.

3 Daughter of R. W. Elston, who might have built Michigan's first successful gasoline-powered automobile "battery operated, capable of running 12 miles an hour on a level road," according to George S. May of Eastern Michigan University.

A *Courier* headline extols that happening—

"THE NEW BEACH HOTEL IS A PARADISE FOR SUMMER VISITORS "

It was also paradise for local workmen who were able to find employment through the long winter months. [1]

Besides the hotel, there were suites available in any one of the 14 white frame cottages along Dixon Avenue. Both cottages and hotel were decorated with massive geranium-filled flower boxes and hanging baskets of petunias. Solid wicker furniture was grouped on freshly painted porches. Rooms were furnished in simple, sturdy rustic or oak. Walls were gaily papered and sheer white curtains with chintz draperies covered the windows. The total effect was crisp, clean and cool.

This is the architect's sketch of the 1915 addition of the Beach Hotel. Architect Clarence Hatzfeld of Chicago had entire charge of the construction of the building from the start to the completion.

"Planned as it is, over the slope of the beach, extending up above the shores of Lake Michigan, seven stories high, with continuous balconies on all the lower five floors, and smaller private balconies on the two upper floors, the hotel makes a most wonderful impression."

Collection of Robert Miles

1 Carpenters were paid 15 cents an hour.

What kind of woman was Martha Baker, really? Again, according to the *Courier*, we learn that she was "a woman of fixed convictions arrived at by careful study of conditions. She achieved her success by the hard road of experience. Her executive ability, her great judgement in the final prevalence of what was right, her tremendous energy and calm judgement gave her ultimate success, as results are figured. Her life was clean and wholesome. . ."

And she left an estate valued at over half a million dollars at her untimely death. Not bad, even before woman's lib —

Martha Baker was adored by her guests and she in turn couldn't do enough for their amusement and comfort. When a group departed on a day's fishing trip by boat on Lake Charlevoix, she'd personally see to it that there was a little surprise treat in each individual box lunch.

The Beach Hotel was one of many popular resort hotels mushrooming in the north thanks to the expanding network of railroads. There was hardly an American town or village at this time beyond the earshot of the whistle of the steam engine or, as it was frequently referred to, the iron horse. In 1896, the railroad built the fashionable Inn on Lake Charlevoix with lumber it bought and hauled from nearby Central Lake at $5.00 per thousand feet.[1] Some thirty years later, at the height of the fashionable tourist season, the Pere Marquette's "Resort Special" became an every day occurrence, transporting passengers to and from Charlevoix to Grand Rapids, Detroit, St. Louis, Cincinnati, and Chicago.

1 During the 1884 season alone, 14,760,500 feet of hard lumber was shipped out from this area.

Tourists streamed into Charlevoix not only by train but by boat as well. The *S. S. Manitou*, Queen of the Great Lakes, owned by the Northern Michigan Transportation Co., was over 300 feet long, and her popular young Captain, William Finucan, prided himself to "always be on time — as exact as the highest class railroad train." The luxurious *Manitou*[1] carried passengers and autos overnight from Chicago to Charlevoix three times a week. Aboard ship, the service was elegant, the staterooms immaculate and the food marvelous. There were always white tablecloths and fresh flowers on the dining room tables.

One of the passengers aboard the *Manitou* was Jules Stein, then a medical student at the University of Chicago. Now he's Chairman of the Board of MCA.[2] In the summer of 1919, this young entrepreneur supplied the Beach Hotel with "six competent musicians for nine weeks." He recalls Mrs. Baker as being a "tough trader." According to the contract, Stein's orchestra was required to play every day including Sunday, not to exceed 26 hours weekly; board and room were included. Mr. Stein wrote me a letter recently, "It is strange to think that I could supply six musicians for the sum of $135.00 a week plus transportation — and still make a profit!"[3]

---

1 Sometimes called the "Greyhound of the Great Lakes." In the Belvedere Club, Ruth Ware notes, — "Chester Morehead brought his movie star bride, Constance Bennett, to the Belvedere for a brief sojourn at the Morehead cottage. . . the bride and groom arrived on the *S. S. Manitou* from Chicago. When glamorous Connie whipped out a cigarette and lit it, Ruth was stunned! That had never happened before in the Belvedere. . ."

2 Music Corporation of America.

3 Additional profit came to him from the contractual revenues received from providing personnel for the barber shop and beauty parlor for the hotel.

Beauty Parlor and Barber Shop

Charlevoix Beach Hotel

for the Convenience of Our Guests. Beauty Parlor and Barber Shop completely equipped — with thoroughly experienced operators.

Operated by Shops of Service Chicago, Illinois

He must have made a nice profit because he returned in 1920 to supervise a benefit for the Charlevoix Hospital's new ambulance.

> "There will be a cotillion with numerous favors for everyone; a large silver cup for the best dancers. . . Mrs. J. S. Baker has turned over the entire hotel for the occasion. . . and it is expected that everyone will be there." [1]

"Everyone" surely included people of substance who expected the best and were willing to pay for it without any qualms. This included such prominent Jewish families as E. J. Block (Inland Steel) and Albert Loeb (Sears Roebuck) from Chicago; David May (Department Stores) from St. Louis; Cy Lazarus (Federated Department Stores) from Dayton, Ohio; J. Godchaux (sugar) and Albert Wachenheim, Sr. (shoes) from New Orleans.

Another charity event, supported not only by the "northsiders" but by the Belvedere and Chicago Clubs as well, is described as follows:

1 *Charlevoix Courier*, Aug. 1919.

"The grand ball of the season was held in the Inn ballroom for the benefit of the Charlevoix Hospital, Saturday evening, Aug. 7. Dancing started at 8:30 and lasted until 11:30. There were hundreds present, beautifully frocked ladies and society from all sides of Charlevoix — Belvedere, Chicago Club, Beach, Pine Lake and inside. The cottages were well represented also."[1]

Not to be out-done, the annual Charlevoix Chauffeur's Ball proved to be equally successful in behalf of the local hospital. The dance was given by both the hometown chauffeurs and the summer ones as well. Jules Stein's "jazz band" from the Beach Hotel "made a big hit with the crowd!"

Nor were the young people overlooked. "Thirty-five college and university students from 14 colleges and universities were entertained at the Congregational parsonage for an 'Acquaintance Social.' These young people have been employed at the Beach and Belvedere hotels and Chicago Club during the summer. They passed a pleasant evening singing songs, doing 'stunts' and winding up with a marshmallow roast." [2]

The year 'round residents who lived inside of town or what is referred to as the "valley," often found themselves in a bind — dependent on the summer people for business, yet resentful of this dependency. And although the *Charlevoix Courier* repeatedly advised local merchants and tradesmen that "the secret of the tourist proposition is hospitality," some surprising hidden prejudices came to the fore in this front page article.

---

1 *Charlevoix Courier*, Aug. 1919.

2 *Charlevoix Courier*, Aug. 29, 1917.

"The Valley has at last come into its own! No longer will its residents have to knuckle down to the haughty northsiders and the fastidious Belvederians, turning their faces to the north and east like the Turk at prayer. For the valley is to have a restaurant and club just about four or five jumps ahead of anything of its kind in the region. . ."

And then this enthusiastic article amazingly concludes,

"This will meet with instant approval and hearty support of our summer visitors."[1]

But in spite of such incredible public relations, the future looked bright for Mrs. Baker. She had great plans for the Beach Hotel. Guests were booking reservations from one year to the next. Blueprints were ready which included 135 more rooms with baths, a dining room with the seating capacity of 700 people, a tea room for 200 and the installation of a large pipe organ in the Casino.

Unfortunately, none of this came about.

During the winter of 1922, Martha Baker died in Miami, Florida, of cancer.[2] In her will, made out the month before, she left her husband John the "Riverside" cottage and the hotel laundry. To her daughter, Doris Von Dolcke, she left the hotel (including a $145,000 mortgage with the Detroit Trust Co.) and the remainder of her property.

John Baker, Martha's husband, was a retired blacksmith. His great claim to fame seems to have been the ability to grind up a whiskey glass in his mouth after consuming the contents. And daughter Doris? A fun-loving girl. People say when she was in a

1 *Charlevoix Courier*

2 Martha Baker was born in 1865 in Exeter, Ontario. She lies buried in Brookside Cemetary, Charlevoix.

gay mood, she'd invite the whole orchestra from the Beach to a nearby gambling club in Harbor Springs. One of the desk clerks recalls seeing her waltz into the lobby "higher than a kite" at 6 a.m. waving her dancing shoes above her head.

Doris Baker married Arthur Von Dolcke,[1] and whether the decline of the Beach over the next few years was a result of their combined inefficiency or the Depression is hard to judge. Probably both factors entered into the financial eclipse of the Beach. Gradually, gone were Chef Jones and the attentive porter who knew every guest by name; the charming social director from Washington, D.C.; the competent secretary; the smiling college bellboys. Suddenly pampered guests were expected to carry their own luggage. Their rings for room service went unanswered.

In a desperate last ditch stand to make a go of the Hotel, Von Dolcke invited a Detroit gambler to open a gambling club on the lower level, with the house claiming 40 percent of the profits.

Ironically the theme of the last social party given at the Beach during the late 50's was a Prohibition dinner-dance with all cocktails served in tea cups. Somehow the local police took a dim view of the gambling-drinking arrangements (Michigan is fussy about this sort of thing), and so they staged an honest-to-goodness RAID. The guests, of course, thinking this all a part of the party atmosphere, paid no attention to the hostess' frantic signals. Instead they toasted her in greatest admiration with, "To our clever hostess!"

---

1 The late Earl Young, Charlevoix's historian, recalled that Arthur Von Dolcke's uncle was the attending physician when Lincoln was shot. The Lincoln family, in gratitude, gave the doctor a handsome cane with inlaid silver scenes of Lincoln's life. This cane eventually came into possession of Von Dolcke, who sold it to a guest at the Beach Hotel.

CHARLEVOIX BEACH HOTEL
Charlevoix, Michigan

Cocktail Lounge

COCKTAILS

French 75	.75	Alexander	.50
Champagne Cocktail	.75	Rob Roy	.50
Daquiri	.50	Bronx	.45
Bacardi	.50	Dubonnet	.45
Scarlett O'Hara	.50	Pink Lady	.40
Rhett Butler	.50	Manhattan	.40
Stinger	.50	Old Fashioned	.40
Side Car	.50	Orange Blossom	.40
	Martini	.35	

FIZZES and COLLINS

Planters Punch	.60	Cuba Libre	.45
Mint Julep	.60	Whiskey Sour	.40
Singapore Sling	.50	Orange Gin Collins	.40
Rum Collins	.45	Mint Gin Collins	.40
Sloe Gin Fizz	.45	Tom Collins	.35
	Gin Rickey	.35	

RUMS

Myer's "Planters Punch"		Bacardi Gold Label	.50
Rum	.50	Bacardi Silver Label	.40
	Ron Rico Gold Label	.40	

SCOTCH

Haig & Haig, Pinch	.50	Vat 69	.45
Johnnie Walker Black Label	.50	Dewar's White Label	.45
Ballantines	.50	Teachers	.45
Cutty Sark	.50	Black & White	.45
White Horse	.45	King William IV	.45

BRANDIES

Hennessy	.50	Martell	.50

WHISKEY

Canadian Club	.45	Seagrams, V. O.	.45
Old Grand-Dad	.45	Old Overholt, Rye	.40
Mt. Vernon, Rye	.45	Sunny Brook	.35
Old Taylor	.45	Century Club, Rye	.35

GINS

Gordon's	.35	Sloe Gin	.35
Mint Gin	.35	John Collins	.30
Orange Gin	.35	Hiram Walker	.30

LIQUEURS

Cointreau S. A. R. L.	.50	Creme de Cocoa	.50
Creme de Menthe, White	.50	Curacao	.50
Creme de Menthe, Green	.50	Blackberry Liqueur	.50
D. O. M. Benedictine	.50	Apricot Liqueur	.50
	Southern Comfort	.45	

SANDWICHES

Beach Club Sandwich	1.00	Imported Swiss	.40
Sliced Chicken	.60	Bacon, Lettuce, Tomato	.35
Virginia Ham	.50	Grilled Cheese	.35

Wines and Champagne

A true friend I've found in Estella
Together we've raised a lot of hella
To you I toast my glass of wine
Because I think you are genuine

Two college girls working as
waitresses at the Inn Hotel.

Two college boys working as bus boys at the Beach Hotel during the summer.

Rumors still persist that toward the end of Prohibition, Detroit's Purple Gang occupied one of the Beach Hotel cottages. If this is true, they stayed incognito and kept out of trouble. However, someone stole the fastest speedboat on the Great Lakes right out of its boathouse in Charlevoix's Round Lake harbor in the dead of winter in '31![1] (Bootleggers? Probably! The Purple Gang's "little navy"? Maybe.) A 26-foot Hacker, built especially for English sportswoman Betty Carstairs, the boat was put at her disposal during Detroit's Gold Cup races.

An old time gambler recalls that Von Dolcke "had a helluva location. He appealed to the carriage trade. There were society women from Chicago who played roulette every afternoon and lost thousands of dollars, but nobody cared. You follow what I mean — they could afford it. A cold club don't work with resorters — only with the sawdust trade. Get what I mean? Resorters loved the dining, dancing and entertainment—not just raw gambling."

It was an unwritten law that not everyone could get into northern Michigan's exclusive gambling clubs. At the Beach, a year-round resident was hired as a "spotter." It was his job to give the nod to those who were eligible for admission (resorters) and exclude those who were not (townies).

Even after the repeal of Prohibition, Von Dolcke's luck with the running of the Beach Hotel didn't improve. In 1939 a fire broke out in the sagging hotel kitchen resulting in $7,500 worth of damage, and the patient Detroit Trust Company foreclosed on the mortgage because "defendant failed utterly to protect the mortgage property by fire insurance. . . and the defendant's incompetent management since 1931 has produced no result except aforesaid waste, series of deficits, neglect of municipal and public utility service obligations, loss of credit among tradesmen and loss of hotel patronage."[2] The Von Dolckes sold out and left town.

---

1 Owned by Julius W. Gilbert of Detroit, Michigan.

2 Excerpt from a Baker cottage abstract.

During the 40's, 50's and 60's the ownership of the decaying hotel bounced back and forth among many owners, each trying to revive its former popularity without success. One owner hired go-go-girls — much to the local ministers' consternation (shades of the "hurdy-gurdy twists and wiggletail glides"!). Another owner catered to ski groups. A third planned razing the old place and building a new hotel with a revolving restaurant on top. Nothing came of these schemes.

Finally, the old place was condemned — the last of its generation to fall under the wreckers' hammer. [1]

While the building was being torn down, a fire again broke out on October 16, 1967. The Beach burned more brightly that night than even during its hey-day when every room sparkled with electricity. A woman who lived across the street sighed with relief the following morning, "This is the first good night's sleep I've had in years. I was always afraid the Beach was going to burn down and now it has!"

The ashes of the hotel presently are being bulldozed along with the debris of the archeological dig recently excavated by scientists from Michigan State University. Sixty-four new condominiums with balconies and tinted windows will face the copper-colored super sunsets over Lake Michigan.

When the La Croft condominiums are completed this year, the new owners will walk along the same beach in the footsteps of earlier resorters from the Beach Hotel, as well as the voyageurs, lumberjacks, fur-traders and Woodland Indians.

Sic transit gloria mundi.

---

1 The Inn Hotel and the Belvedere Resort Hotel had already been torn down.

CONTRACT

Contract for the Charlevoix Beach Hotel, Charlevoix, Michigan
Party of the first part, Mrs. J.S.Baker,
Party of the second part, Jules C. Stein

1. The undersigned as party of the first part and second
part respectively, enter into this agreement.
2. The party of the first part leases to the party of
the second part the Beauty Parlor and Barber Shop
within the Charlevoix Beach Hotel for the summer
season of 1920. (Season constitutes from the
opening day to the closing day of said Hotel). The
party of the first part furnishes the respective
rooms; necessary and permanent equipment such as
barber chair; dresseur, chairs, manicuring table,
dresseur, chairs, shampoo board, and the like
equipment. The party of the first part further
agrees to furnish hot water and cold water (running)
and light.
3. In consideration of such lease the party of the
second part agrees to pay to the party of the first
part the sum of $150. payable as follows:
$75. on July 15, 1920
$75 on August 15, 1920
4. The party of the first part agrees to room
the operators in said shops for $3.50 each weekly
and to board the operators for $14. weekly each.
5. It is agreed that no deduction shall be made
on any account except for flood, fire, or act of
providence.

In testimony whereof we have affixed our hands
and seals this _12_ day of _Dec_,1919

Martha R. Baker
Party of the first part

Jules Stein
Party of the second part

CONTRACT

Contract for, Charlevoix Beach Hotel,
Charlevoix, Michigan
Party of the first part, Mrs. J.S.Baker
Party of the second part, Jules C. Stein

1. The undersigned, as party of the first part
and second part respectively, enter into this
agreement.
2. The party of the second part agrees to furnish
the services of _five_ thoroughly competent
musicians for the party of the first part for
a period of approximately nine (9) weeks
commencing on or about ___July 10,___ 1920, the
stipulations of said service shall be as follows:
The said orchestra is to play every day including
Sunday, for said period of approximately nine (9)
weeks, hours not to exceed twenty-six (26) weekly.
Hours to be divided as per arrangements .
3. Said orchestra is to receive proper board and
lodging as furnished by said management, as of
season 1919.
4. For such services the party of the first part
agrees to pay to the party of the second part
the sum of One Hundred and _fifty five_ dollars,
$155., weekly, said sum payable the day following
the close of each week.
5.The party of the first part agrees to pay
complete transportation for said orchestra from
Chicago Illinois to Charlevoix, Michigan and
from Charlevoix Michigan to Chicago, Illinois.at
Said transportation to Charlevoix Michigan to
be advanced on July 1, 1920 Return transportation
to be paid at close of engagement.
6. It is further agreed that no deduction shall
be made on any account except fire, flood, or
act of providence.

In testimony of the above we have affixed our hands
and seals this _13th._ day of ___March___ 1920

Mrs. J.S Baker
Party of the first part

Jules C. Stein
Party of the second part

The dig. A Michigan State University archeology team spent the summer of '71 and spring of '72 digging in three feet of dirt for Indian relics. Carefully.

Photo by Fred Davison for the Detroit Free Press, 1972.

Editorial page
Charlevoix COURIER

Charlevoix Courier, Wednesday, February 9, 1972 Page 9

Archeologist Must Work Fast to Save Charlevoix Artifacts

Dr. Charles Clelland of Michigan State University has a problem which touches all of us in the city of Charlevoix.

As an archeologist, Dr. Clelland has spent many years probing into man's prehistoric past, sifting the ruins of ancient villages and trying to discover how life was lived in the American wilderness centuries before the arrival of the white man.

One of the richest archeological digs he has found is located at the foot of W. Dixon-ave. on the site of the former Holiday Beach Hotel.

Dr. Clelland and his workers from MSU spent several days at the site last summer and uncovered a wealth of pottery shards and flint tools used by Woodland Indians who inhabited the area 1,000 years ago.

They also found remnants of a civilization which apparently flourished in the area about 3,000 years ago -- 1,000 years before Christ.

Dr. Clelland has planned to make a thorough study of the site, possibly spanning several years, but suddenly time is of the essence.

Ralph Hess has announced plans to construct a condominium on the location, with construction starting in June.

Dr. Clelland would like to spend several weeks this spring at the site before the builders move in to recover as many relics of those by-gone days as possible.

City Superintendent Thomas Hanna has offered the use of city equipment in removing the fill dirt that was dumped on the site after the hotel was torn down.

But Dr. Clelland still needs about $2,000 to pay his workers and funds for the Charlevoix archeological project at MSU are depleted.

Charlevoixans interested in preserving something of that long-gone era when roving bands of nomads camped on our shores are asked to make their contributions to the Charlevoix Archeological Project, Michigan State University, in care of Dr. Charles Clelland.

Just think! For three thousand years -- possibly longer -- folks have found Charlevoix a pleasant place to live!

As a result of this appeal, over $2,500 was received from Charlevoix citizens to help with the dig, which is located on the site of the former Beach Hotel.

November 22, 1975

PROGRESS REPORT OF THE PINE RIVER CHANNEL SITE
by
Margaret Holman
Michigan State University

It is becoming clear as analysis of the Pine River Channel Site progresses further that its importance for answering questions about Michigan's prehistory has not been underestimated. To date, attention has focused on analysis of the pottery, projectile points, and plant remains. The results of this research are that changes through time in the study area are being better understood and that ideas concerning the Pine River Channel Site being occupied during the warm season are being borne out. In addition, the site will prove a useful guide for other sites recently excavated in the Inland Waterway of northern Lower Michigan.

The pottery at the Pine River Channel Site represents a time span from the late Middle Woodland (ca. A.D. 400 - A.D. 600) through the Late Woodland, ca. A.D. 1000 - A.D. 1600, though the bulk of it dates between A.D. 600 and A.D. 1100. This is called the early Late Woodland, a portion of which was previously defined at the Juntunen Site on Boise Blanc Island and termed the Mackinac Phase of the Late Woodland by Alan MacPherron in 1967. The Mackinac Phase at this site lasted from ca. A.D. 800 to A.D. 1000 and includes pottery called Mackinac Ware. Mackinac Ware constitutes a large portion of the pottery at the Pine River Channel Site, and, more importantly, there is a new variety of pottery which we now call Pine River Ware. This pottery was the variety made in the 200-year period between the late Middle Woodland and the Mackinac Phase. Because Pine River Ware has characteristics of both the earlier and later ceramics at the site, a continuous sequence has been established that suggests the site was occupied successively by essentially the same group of people. This situation helps to answer the question of the origins of the Late Woodland in northwest Lower Michigan. It can now be said that the Late Woodland culture in the area was of local origins and was not brought to northern Lower Michigan by outside peoples. The nature of the changes that took place remains a problem to be considered as analysis continues. It is expected that the period of time from A.D. 600 to A.D. 800, which is represented ceramically by Pine River Ware and which is called the Pine River Phase, will be crucial in this regard, because it is a time when Late Woodland patterns of environmental exploitation, settlement, and social organization were being developed.

Results of both the pottery and projectile point analysis indicates the direction of trade or other kinds of contact between the prehistoric occupants of Charlevoix and other groups in the Great Lakes area. During the Middle Woodland occupation, there is a suggestion of interaction with the Illinois region because of the presence of a potsherd of the Havana Middle Woodland Tradition of Illinois and another that is imitative of central Illinois decorative style ceramics. In addition, there is a corner-notched projectile point, which is a type common to the Middle Woodland and which is made on flint, that is definitely not found in Michigan but is similar to the Burlington chert of the lower Illinois Valley.

Likewise, relationships with Wisconsin are indicated by both pottery and projectile points. Thus a side-notched point was found that was possibly of Wisconsin oolitic chert as well as a portion of a pottery vessel of the type Aztalan Collared from the Aztalan Site in Wisconsin. The Aztalan Site dates around A.D. 1100 to A.D. 1300, so this vessel was brought to the Pine River Channel Site during the Late Woodland.

Charred plant seeds from the site, recovered by a process known as flotation, have been examined by Ms. Nancy Nowak, a graduate student specializing in paleobotany at Michigan State University. Several plants occur that are documented historically as being used by native peoples. These include raspberry or blackberry (*Rubus* spp.), lambsquarter (*Chenopodium album*), hawthorn (*Crataegus* spp.), and elder (*Sambucus canadensis*). Two other kinds of plants were found. These were dock (*Rumex* spp.) and leadplant or indigo-bush amorpha (*Amorpha* spp.). All of these plant species are available during the late summer and early autumn, especially August and September. Only one, dock (*Rumex* spp.) is available as early as May. On the basis of the plant remains then, it can be said that the Pine River Channel Site was probably occupied at least during the late summer and early fall. Additional evidence of seasonality will be obtained when the animal bone is identified.

The question of the season of occupation at the Pine River Channel Site is important because in attempting to discover how native peoples utilized the products of their environment, it is necessary to know how sites were located with relation to the seasonal availability of various resources and how patterns of activity within a site might reflect the use of the environment. It has been postulated that during the Late Woodland, people lived in relatively large summer villages along the Lake Michigan coast in order to take advantage of fishing possibilities. In the winter these villages broke up into smaller family groups that moved inland to hunt. Indications that the Pine River Channel Site and other sites on the coast are warm season occupations tend to confirm part of this hypothesis. In order to see if winter sites were located in the interior, Michigan State University crews directed by Dr. Charles E. Cleland and Dr. William A. Lovis spent the summers of 1974 and 1975 locating and excavating sites along the Inland Waterway from the Petoskey area to Cheboygan. The Pine River Channel Site will be compared with these other sites to see if differences in kinds of tools, house patterns, site size, as well as animal and plant differences reflect different portions of the seasonal round.

Finally, it is hoped that the single radiocarbon date of A.D. 1035 ± 80 on a Mackinac Phase vessel from the Pine River Channel Site can be supplemented by more dates.

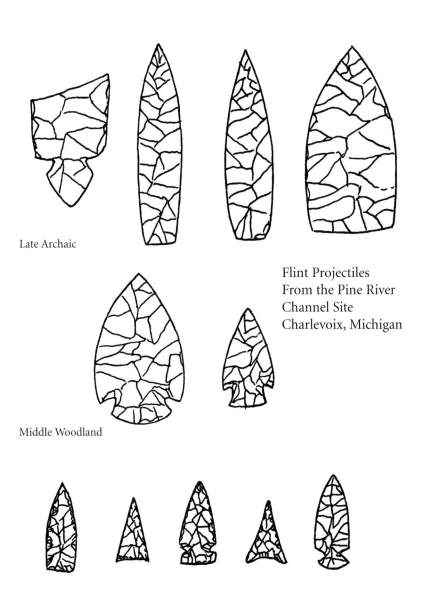

Late Archaic

Flint Projectiles
From the Pine River
Channel Site
Charlevoix, Michigan

Middle Woodland

Late Woodland

Charlevoix Courier, August 1920

Two Ways of Playing Ball

SUNDAY'S GAME PROVED TO BE AN EXCEPTION

Two Thousand Spectators Witness
Game Between Charlevoix and
Loeb Farms League Teams

Charlevoix baseball fans witnessed a game of ball between the Loeb Farms team and the Charlevoix city team on Sunday last that will leave a lasting impression on their minds, clearly demonstrating two methods of playing this national game — as it has been played in previous games and as it was played on Sunday last.

Baseball as it should be played is good clean sport and when played in any other manner, is not only a disgrace to the community, but disgusting to the average spectator. From all we can learn, Sunday's game came under the latter classification.

Trouble was apparently brewing from the time the first ball crossed the home plate, and reached a climax in the ninth inning. Men of average intelligence apparently lost their heads and only the efforts of those who were real sportsmen prevented a free-for-all fight.

The list of casualties, as the game proceeded, grew to proportions that compared favorably with a southern race riot, and had it continued many innings more, our local hospital would have been filled to capacity.

Friends of years are friends no more. Charges of unfair methods and bribery were exchanged, with or without foundation. Can this be baseball? We think not.

THE CASUALTIES

Hinckley, Charlevoix catcher, ankle spiked and fingers split.

Frank Newasic, Loeb Farms 1st baseman, both bones of leg broken between knee and ankle.

Whiteford, umpire, hit in ear by foul tip.

Leon Foster, catcher for Loebs, hit on forehead by foul tip, knocked unconscious for fifteen or twenty minutes, remaining in a semi-unconscious condition for several hours.

Two spectators hit by foul balls and more or less hurt.

The game ended in the eleventh inning. Score 10 to 8 in favor of Loeb Farms. Spectators estimated that 2,000 witnessed the game.

As a result, Sunday baseball in Charlevoix is being looked upon in an unfavorable light by many, including those who were opposed to it as well as those who were in favor of it. The reason is apparent, and as long as men of mature age and judgement lose control of themselves as some did at last Sunday's game, not only Sunday ball but all ball games will be looked upon with disfavor. Play the game as gentlemen or keep away. "Don't be a ragchewer; look how the moth is despised."

Historic Loeb Farms
Charlevoix Showplace

Loeb Farms   Photo by Robert Miles in the early 30's

The LOEB FARMS, built in 1918, was a show place in its heyday. This model experimental dairy and horse farm in its storybook setting of steep-roofed buildings, dormers, cupolas, towers, and flying buttresses was a lively place to be on a Saturday afternoon. Here people could watch a ballgame, buy ice cream, cheese, or flowers, or just stop to see the registered livestock quartered in palatial surroundings with the latest inventions in Sears, Roebuck equipment. There were about 90 people on the payroll, who cared for the fields, animals, gardens, and orchards.

Ernest Hemingway Guest at Baseball Game

"We had a softball team that often challenged the 'natives' to a contest. I recall in 1917 or 1918 we had such a game on a vacant lot . . . The team was free to use any resorter on Pine Lake (Lake Charlevoix) and we always tried to get Bill Smith of Horton's Bay. Bill came to pitch that day and brought with him a guest named Ernest Hemingway. Hemingway was limping quite badly so we let him play first base — the slowman's spot. After the game we learned that this guy Hemingway's leg was full of shrapnel he received while in the Ambulance Service in Italy during the War."[1]

Ernest Hemingway, Nobel prize winning author, as a youth in Horton Bay.
Photo courtesy Jon Hartwell

1 Belvedere Club 1969. Joe Bohrer.

The Red Fox Inn
by
Edith Gilbert
(*Charlevoix Courier*, March 1, 1995)

You may wonder why the National Register of Historic Places has just listed the RED FOX INN on the Boyne City Road as worthy of preservation.

There are many good reasons. For one, Ernest Hemingway was a familiar face in the kitchen of the popular restaurant. Legend has it that the owner, Vollie Fox, taught young Hemingway how to fish, and when Hemingway returned to Horton Bay in 1919 after being wounded in Italy, he gave a World War I helmet to Vollie Fox's nine year old son, Raymond. Vollie's sister-in-law wrote in her diary in May, "Saw Ernest (sic) Hemingway who was severely wounded in Italy. Has 237 wounds. One leg stiff, one kneecap gone, but looks fine now."

Long before the RED FOX INN became a favorite of Charlevoix's fashionable summer crowd, the building served as a boarding house for lumbermen and transient guests. It was built in 1878 and still has the wavy, irregular glass double hung windows.

The idea of opening a restaurant in 1919, according to historian William Ohle, resulted from a successful dinner which the Foxes put on at the Inn for wealthy summer visitors from St. Louis, the Alvin Goldmans. Mrs. Goldman is credited with giving Mrs. Fox the recipe for tomato pudding, which helped to make the restaurant famous. Years later, Mrs. Goldman shared this recipe with me, and you will find it in my book, *All About Parties*. Fried chicken, freshly picked corn on the cob, dumplings, cheese rolls, and other 'fixings', such as relishes, pickles and strawberry jam accounted for families making annual pilgrimages to this remote white-painted, clapboard building.

The first floor of the Inn still has a distinguished-looking forty-five foot porch where guests could have a cocktail before dinner — if they brought their own liquor. There were three small dining rooms, and in the back were several summer kitchens — a salad room, a main kitchen, a dishwashing room, the dumpling room, the pickle room and the chauffeurs' room. The latter was reserved exclusively for the drivers of the well-to-do resorters.

The first time I was taken to the Red Fox Inn by my father-in-law, Sam Gilbert, a cigar manufacturer, I recall that he brought a box of R.G. Dunn cigars to Vollie Fox. In exchange, and according to tradition, Vollie gave Sam some freshly caught brook trout. We celebrated many birthdays and anniversaries during the summer months at this charming little restaurant. One must remember, too, that in those early days, there was no other dining competition, except perhaps the gambling casino, Koch's. Most summer people frequently entertained at home and borrowed each other's staff for large occasions.

In 1955, Mrs. Fox sold the Inn to her daughter, Marian Hartwell, who ran the restaurant very ably until the '70's. Since then, her son, James, operates the property as a bed and breakfast inn during the warm-weather months. You will notice little change in the appearance either inside or out in recent years of either the Inn or the town of Horton Bay. Nestled in a grove of pine, the interior of the Inn is filled with the original furniture, mirrors and pictures from those long ago days described by Hemingway in his first book published in 1923, *Three Stories and Ten Poems*. "Horton Bay, the town was only five houses on the main road between Boyne City and Charlevoix. There was a general store and a post office with a high false front and maybe a wagon hitched out in front, Smith's house, Stroud's house, Fox's house, Horton's house and Van Hoosen's house."

Today, the quaint town of Horton Bay lays its claim to fame by the annual, humorous and well publicized Fourth of July parade. Its inhabitants have also capitalized on clinging to the nostalgic quality of its early history, and that is another reason the Red Fox Inn deserves to be preserved on the National Register of Historic Places.

* * *

Julia Scott,
Where Are You?

by
Edith Gilbert
(*Detroit Free Press*, February 13, 1971)

The people down in Lansing don't have the feel of Michigan Avenue — and how could they?

To the Department of State Highways, Michigan Avenue is nothing more than a name of a short street a few blocks long in a pretty northern Michigan summer resort named Charlevoix.

Chances are they're not aware that the huge white homes along the west side of the street, poised on a bluff, face blazing sunsets from Lake Michigan almost every evening; where in the summer, steep wooden steps zig-zagging to the beach are worn down by five generations of bare feet hauling charcoal and hot dogs to the shore; where small children collect and polish coveted "Petoskey stones" to sell to the tourists; and where at night young adults share dreams of love under the white spotlight of a northern moon.

It's a street that once echoed the clippety clop of fashionable horse-drawn carriages. A few old-timers still recall seeing Julia Scott, great-great aunt of Adlai Stevenson III, riding up Michigan Avenue at the turn of the century, driven by a local coachman behind two black horses.

Please don't misunderstand — the street is not run down now just because it's old! On the contrary, Michigan Avenue is a well-preserved dowager, surrounded by loving progeny eager to serve her beck and call.

This was proven during the recent ruckus — but I'm getting ahead of my story.

These days, glancing through my living room window, I see Charlevoixans cruising along the block slowly, each car filled with curious out-of-town visitors. Invariably the driver pauses and points out lovely three-story mansions flanked by green lawns and shaded by ancient maple trees.

At this moment I can hear the hammering from across the street where workmen are busy renovating and winterizing the home built originally in 1917 for Colonel Beaumont, brother-in-law of the founder of the May Department Stores.[1] (The bill to paint the inside and outside of the house then was only $5,000. Today, one estimate for the same job is $25,000 — an offer quickly turned down by the new owner, Thomas A. Duke of Farmington, Michigan.)

And it is here on this spot in front of this white-pillared Duke mansion that a most remarkable sidewalk confrontation took place between formidable Julia Scott and the local establishment over half a century ago.

But first let me tell you a little about Mrs. Mathew T. Scott and her sister, Mrs. Adlai Stevenson I. A Kentucky-born

---

1 See photo page 85.

Democrat, Julia Scott gained national prestige when she was elected first President General of the D.A.R. (Daughters of the American Revolution) — and what a revolutionary she was! She served in this office for four years and personally directed the development and construction of the beautiful D.A.R. Memorial Building in Washington, D.C., where her portrait and that of her sister, Mrs. Stevenson I[1] (the second D.A.R. President General), hang in the Illinois Room.

During World War I, Mrs. Scott was decorated by the French Ambassador in Washington at a special ceremony in her honor for her magnificent leadership in war work. One of the guests at the ceremony in the French Embassy described her eloquent response to the Ambassador's citation as a masterpiece.

The spirit of Julia Scott guards her beloved knoll where the sidewalk confrontation took place.

Photo by Tony Spina, *Detroit Free Press,* 1971

1 Mrs. Adlai Ewing Stevenson was the kind of woman who refused Ulysses S. Grant's request for a whiskey with a gentle, "We don't serve spirits in our home, but do have a lemonade."

But Washington, D.C., and Bloomington, Illinois[1] were unbearably hot without air-conditioning during the humid months, and people like Mrs. Scott and those of her acquaintance fled the heat to breathe the pure fresh air of northern Michigan. Sugar tycoons from as far as New Orleans, industrialists and assorted millionaires from Chicago, St. Louis, and Baltimore arrived by boat and train in Charlevoix with their families, servants, pets, briefcases, trunks, and yes — sometimes even mistresses — the latter discreetly stashed away in near-by resort hotels.

During the summer of 1918, when the sidewalk confrontation between Mrs. Scott and the local establishment takes place, World War I is drawing to a spectacular close. The local weekly *Charlevoix Courier* is urging women to register for national defense on the one hand while cautioning them on the other to beware of making dandelion wine because Michigan under a new set of laws is now a completely dry state. Truman H. Newberry is running for U.S. Senator from Michigan, and in a column entitled "The Weekly Tip," written by the Caddie Master of the Golf Club, he suggests it may be necessary this summer to hire girl caddies! A good part of the paper, including the front page, is taken up with "Letters from Overseas," and unless there was an insufficient number of Council Members present, there are the usual notices and reports of the meetings of the City Council.

---

1. *The Belvedere Club.* 1969. Elizabeth Ives. "Picnics were important social events. The Annual Bloomington Picnic called for two or more buses with seats running along the side so everyone faced each other. At the rear were three steps and we jumped off and on. The big heavy horses didn't make much speed to Michigan Beach. The only serious quarrel I found between mother and father in the old letters I have gone through, was my father scolding mother for staying on Michigan Beach with Lydiard Horton (our house guest and a great philosopher) "until 9:30 at night, Helen, and this I can't forgive." I gather father was pretty jealous not to be in Charlevoix; he was helping his own father in his campaign for Governor of Illinois in 1908 (Adlai Stevenson I)."

Photo of Julia Scott and her cottage, The Wilds. Extensive remodeling was done in 1975 because the structure sagged 8". Over 600 ft. of steel beams were installed on three levels. During this remodeling phase, the date 1897 was found penciled on a piece of lumber.

Photo by Tony Spina, *Detroit Free Press*, 1971

Long before World War I, around the turn of the century, nature lover, conservationist Julia Scott purchased her secluded summer cottage and named it "The Wilds." In 1905 the street was not paved, there were no sidewalks, and the simple wooden cottage, set back behind a tempting knoll, was hidden from the road by numerous trees and a clutch of raspberry bushes. The following year, 1906, she purchased the adjoining wooded knoll for $250, ensuring her complete privacy. As the years rolled by, she enhanced the rustic flavor of "The Wilds" by planting ferns shipped from England, and it was one of the provisions when the house was sold by her heirs that the English ferns would be retained.

Here in this rustic setting, Mrs. Scott spent many idyllic summers with her two daughters, Julia and Lititia, and her house-keeper-companion, Mary Hunter. Pleasant days these. Lolling in a hammock. Breathing the cool air off the lake. Sometimes dictating letters to the editor of *The New York Times*. Buggy riding in the country to locate fresh corn on the cob. Giving great tea parties where refreshing, non-alcoholic punch was served from chilled cut glass bowls. Sometimes her guest list included William Davis, grandfather of Adlai Stevenson II, who all had a summer cottage at the nearby Belvedere Club; or a Michigan Avenue neighbor, Sara Teasdale, Pulitzer Prize winning poetess; or such dignitaries from Washington, D.C., as Thomas Marshall, Vice-President of the United States under Woodrow Wilson. (This Veep's claim to fame stems from his remark that what this country really needs is a good five-cent cigar!)

Marshall was a friend of Carl Vrooman, Assistant Secretary of Agriculture under Woodrow Wilson and married to Julia Scott's daughter and namesake. Julia Vrooman, a lovely lady now in her 90's and, according to Adlai II, one of the wittiest women in the whole world, completed a popular novel, *The High Road to Honor*, at the Charlevoix cottage in 1918. She recalls the time her mother invited all the D.A.R. delegates from Ohio and Illinois to Charlevoix, but somehow word spread, and before she knew it, people from all over the United States appeared. The family thought the walls would burst apart, but the staunch little cottage survived this reception and many other functions, including a small family outdoor wedding in August, 1922. Here on the lawn, overlooking a brilliant Lake Michigan sunset, Mrs. Scott's grand-daughter, Mildred Bromwell, was married to Captain Bailey of London. (And in August, 1970, the present owners of "The Wilds" again held a family wedding—for their grandson—in exactly the same natural setting. Although the setting today is still beautiful, the view, some people feel, is not as grandiose since the comple-tion of the Medusa Portland Cement Plant on the south point of the bay and it certainly hasn't improved the quality of the air Mrs. Scott valued so highly, even though Charlevoix Township has recently passed the most restrictive regulations for air pollution in the United States.)

When looking back at Mrs. Scott's life-style between the two World Wars, one can't help but marvel at the contrasts when elegance and simplicity held hands. What simplicity? For one thing — no closets. Clothes were hung on hooks in the bedrooms. The kitchen had no running water, only a hand pump. Instead of gas or electricity there was a wood-burning stove. On cool days in September (there was no rush getting the girls back to school) the house was heated by a wood furnace and the grate fires were laid with 4 ft. logs. The small room off the front hall which is now a powder room was the tool room where gardening equipment was stored.

So much for simplicity. What elegance? One can almost hear Mrs. Scott saying to her butler, "George, hand me a rake !" Mark Smith, author of the novel *The Middleman*, lived on Michigan Avenue in his youth and describes the street colorfully. "The summer way of life as I knew it was to go out with the limousines and chauffeurs, the maids and cooks and nurses,who on a sunny day would paint the streets of the town with the colors of their uniforms."

Much of the fine wicker furniture is still in the house along with some delicate china plates hanging on the dining room wall and an attic full of books that the present owners, the William Ockrants of Cincinnati, have never gotten around to sorting.

Mrs. Scott's mail was delivered by Dan McSauba, a man without a drop of Scotch blood in him. Dan's real name sounds like Ah-mick-ga-za-bee, which in the Ottawa language means "Submerging Beaver." When early settlers cleared the land along Michigan Avenue to dig foundations for homes among the birches and maples, Dan, a well-educated Indian, noted, "Many Indians lie here — some big chiefs."

This may be so. We know the Indians like to bury their dead high on a bluff, overlooking the fresh waters they dearly love. And because they want their loved ones to sleep in peace, undisturbed, these graves are never groomed.

The Indians, under a Government Grant in August, 1875, were deeded many acres of land along the shore, and the Scott property specifically was deeded to the last of the great Ottawa Chiefs, Shaw-waw-ne-pay-se, meaning "Southern Partridge." Actually, the entire shoreline along Lake Michigan, including the Medusa Cement Plant property, had been promised to the Indians in this area by an earlier treaty. However, somebody didn't read the fine print, and since the Indians believed the land, sky and waters belonged to everyone — the notion of private property was inconceivable to them — the land given them by the United States was sometimes sold for a bag of flour or $1.00 plus other valuable considerations. During 1875-1885 numerous quit claim deeds were recorded, including one to Moses Mic-saw-bay, a relative of Dan McSauba.

Let us now picture Mrs. Scott, swinging in her hand-knotted hammock, reading the *Charlevoix Courier* which Dan has just delivered to her door. It doesn't take much imagination to sense the shock when she comes across the notice that the City Council passed a resolution to provide a sidewalk extending clear to the end of Michigan Avenue — right past "The Wilds"!

A sidewalk!

This means the graceful knoll will be bitten into soon. Ancient trees uprooted. People striding past the secluded cottage. Children bicycling back and forth. The end of peace and quiet and most of all, the end of privacy !

True, there are others who also oppose sidewalk construction here and there around town, for they don't relish the property assessments. Most of the residents go all out, nevertheless, in favor of paving streets and sidewalks, because they're anxious to get rid of the dusty dirt roads that are impassable during heavy rains.

46

Corner of Bridge Street and Antrim Street. In Charlevoix 1898, when the
first sidewalks were installed downtown.

Charlevoix Historical Society

Take the attitude of Charlevoix's mayor at this time, S. M.
Rose, a popular fellow who owns the local barber shop and a
noted sailor who Captains the conservation boat during the summer. He and the Council are mighty proud of the ribbon of concrete beginning to stretch from one end of town to the other. Why,
only a few years before, a delegation was sent to the big city of
Detroit to check on a paved road running all the way from 6 to 7
Mile Road. As a result of this early survey, Charlevoix came to be
one of the first cities in the nation to sport a short concrete paved
road leading downhill from East Dixon Avenue to the picturesque
railroad station. And just to make sure the horses didn't slip, the
paving was indented evenly to look like brick. (If you'd like to see
it, take a look. It's still there.)

Many of these facts are recorded, but there is no record whether Mrs. Scott visited the mayor in his office in the basement of the old Carnegie Library, or mailed him one of her eloquent, fiery letters. She may well have done both. But whichever choice she took, the mayor firmly stood by his decision. Work on the sidewalk will proceed on schedule, he ordered.

"Over my dead body !" answered Julia Scott.

So the day the sidewalk crew arrived with their tools, cement mixers, crushed stone, and sand and proceeded to work their way past the newly completed May and Beaumont "cottages" and up to Julia Scott's precious knoll, she was ready. A neighbor, Richard Lowenstein, recalls the scene. The crew found Mrs. Scott and companion with parasols, camped on her property line, in two chairs beside a table. For convenience there was a pitcher of ice water and two glasses. Regrettably there were no TV trucks present to record the confrontation and we don't know if harsh words and threats or amiable smiles were exchanged that summer day but we do know that up to today there is no sidewalk on the last 200 feet of Michigan Avenue!

Mrs. Scott had won her battle, but that same August, the city fathers passed a strong resolution which, in part, reads as follows: "And it is further resolved that should the above named persons, or any of them neglect or refuse to construct the sidewalk along the line of their respective lands as above described, that the Street Commissioner of the City of Charlevoix proceed to construct said sidewalks in accordance with the provisions of law and the ordinances of said city relative to the construction, maintenance and repairing of sidewalks within the limits of the City of Charlevoix, and the cost and expenses of such construction be assessed upon several places and parcels of land according to law."

And then for many years there was peace and quiet as the status quo of nature lovers was maintained until last summer when Mrs. Scott's beloved knoll was twice threatened.

First, when a neighbor offered to buy 10 feet of the adjoining land in order to build a three-car heated garage. But fortunately the present owner of "The Wilds" refused to sell.

However, the second threat is still pending and is far more serious. Briefly what is happening is this. A beautiful new elementary school recently built on Division Street, which runs into Michigan Avenue, is changing local traffic patterns. As a result, the city applied to the state for funds for paving Division Street. The State Highway engineer recommended that although Michigan Avenue is classified as a major street, it is not functioning effectively because parking is allowed on both sides. Consequently the City Council passed a resolution directing that there be no parking on one side of the street after October 5th, 1970.

This action drives all homeowners to the next council meeting where they plead with the council to let Michigan Avenue revert to a local street and the hell with State funds for paving! They point to the Charlevoix Development Plan, 1970 (financed through a Federal Grant from the Department of Housing and Urban Development). This plan allows the flow of traffic to by-pass Michigan Avenue. A letter is read summing up the feeling of the group. "I have seen what happened in other communities on streets of this type. Originally, there is a beautiful shady drive, lined with lovely homes in a quiet residential street. Then sometime along the way, it is declared a 'major thoroughfare' without any additional changes. Then, later on, it is changed to a 'one-way street.' Still another evolution comes when parking is prohibited on one side of the street. I suggest that the next step will be the logical one. Whereas the State of Michigan has given additional money to Michigan Avenue because it is a 'major thoroughfare' they will then establish a policy here as they have in other communities and say, 'We are in the business of moving traffic and not parking cars.' And at this particular phase you have had it!"

Yes, the people down in Lansing are in business to move traffic and in so doing they may choose to widen Michigan

Avenue. They may decide to cut down the huge maples. They can even tear down Mrs. Scott's beloved knoll, where this morning I saw a deer pause on his way up from his morning swim.

They can do all this and more — I have a feeling Mrs. Scott won't let them! Somehow the eloquent ghost of Mrs. Scott, the revolutionary conservationist, will whisper in a few collective ears, and a little bit of Michigan Avenue will be spared again.

Mrs. Scott's summer cottage, "The Wilds" was the scene of a small, outdoor family wedding in August, 1922. On the lawn overlooking Lake Michigan, Mildred Bromwell, grand-daughter of Julia Scott, married Captain Sidney Baily of London, England.

Mildred Bromwell's daughter, Lady Trenchard, who was born and raised in England, visited Charlevoix for the first time in 1992.

"It is even more beautiful than I thought it would be. You have so many lovely trees and I am very impressed with the color of your blue water. It reminds me of the Mediterranean."

Schooners

(Charlevoix Harbor)

Here by the blue lake harbor
    I watch the ships steam in;
Up the clear wind of morning
    Their smoke climbs black and thin.

Their whistles break the brittle air;
    They beat an angry track;
But oh, the gentle sailing-ships
    That never will come back!

Where is the scarlet *Rosabelle*[1]
    That brought the mill[2] its grain.
Her white sails dripping with the sun,
    Or grayed against the rain?

Where is the *Northern Lady*,
    With cedar logs weighed down,
Whose captain with a wooden leg
    Went clicking up and down?

And the little *Queen of England*,
    That had so fresh an air
When the captain's wife leaned on the rail
    With the sunshine in her hair?

The *Good Squaw* and the *Jasper B.*,
    The Pearl, The Golden Bough –
O gentle ships, O quiet ships,
    Where are you anchored now?

        – Sara Teasdale

1 *The Rosabelle* sank October 30, 1921, during a violent storm on Lake Michigan with the loss of all hands.

2 The mill referred to was the Argo Milling Co. which was located at that time on the present site of the Weathervane Inn.

Sara Teasdale

Sara Teasdale was born in St. Louis in 1884 and died in 1933. Louis Untermeyer said of her, "Reticence walked with her; rudeness died in her presence."

Sara Teasdale, the daughter of John Teasdale, is highly respected in the world of poetry. Her first book, *Sonnets to Duse*, published in 1907, was followed a year later by *Love Songs*, for which she received the Columbia Poetry Society of America Prize, forerunner of the Pulitzer Prize for poetry. She published eight volumes of poetry, the last — *Strange Victory* — appeared in 1933.

Her poetry has a simple, lyric quality. Explaining her poetic theories, she says, "The reader should be barely conscious of the form, the rhymes, or the rhythm. He should be conscious of the emotions given him and unconscious of medium by which they are transmitted . . . The poet should try to give his poem the quiet swiftness of flame, so that the reader will feel and not think while he is reading. But the thinking will come afterwards."

Many of her poems have been set to music. Individual poems have been translated into a number of languages including Danish, French, and Spanish, and there are German and Japanese editions of certain selected poems.

Speaking of the period in which she lived, Sara Teasdale wrote: "For the first time in the history of English literature, the work of women has compared favorably with that of men; and in no other field have they done such noteworthy work as in poetry."

March 17, 1971

Dear Mrs. Gilbert:

I am afraid my memories of Sara Teasdale won't help you much. . . The Teasdales had a wooden lookout which had a wonderful view of north and south points and sometimes several islands. This was reached by a long, railed wooden walk.

One day I saw Miss Teasdale in the lookout, writing. My mother had told me she was a poetess and had read to me a couple of Miss T's poems which I believed had appeared either in the *Atlantic Monthly* or *Harpers*. I wanted a closer look at a poetess so I quietly edged my way toward her. I stopped about twenty feet from her. I was disappointed. She had frizzy pale red hair and freckles and irregular features, a rather sharp face. She looked up and asked, "What do you want, little girl?" I turned and ran. Later I bought every volume of poetry she published but I often wondered who were the lovers she referred to as she didn't look attractive enough to have lovers. Some of her poems I like to think were written on that lookout.

Her father and her mother. . . went for a drive almost every afternoon behind a handsome pair of black horses. They did not have a coachman. . . I believe someone came from the livery stable to hitch and unhitch the horses.

The Teasdales had a low cedar hedge along their front property line. By the hedge grew the first English violets I had seen. They had a lovely odor. My mother had a violet bed behind our house with five or six varieties. I thought she should also have English violets so I pulled up a plant and planted it, but Mama noticed the new plant. I was about to be punished but I persuaded her to let me show her how I had found the plant between the hedge and the walk. I hadn't entered Teasdales' yard . . .

Sincerely,

Laura Jean S. Wulfman (Mrs. E. J.)

DEATH OF AGED SUMMER RESIDENT
John W. Teasdale Succumbs After a
Short Illness

John W. Teasdale of St. Louis, Missouri, died at his home, 303 Michigan Avenue, Sunday morning at 6:00 o'clock, after an illness from the previous Friday, the direct cause of his death being hemmorhage of the stomach.

Mr. Teasdale and wife came to Charlevoix in early June to spend the summer at their cottage, it being his twenty-third season spent in the city. He had been in poor health for some time, but was in hopes that the change of climate would be beneficial to him. He was 82 years old the 13th of last November.

Few among Charlevoix's summer visitors was better known nor enjoyed a larger acquaintance here than Mr. Teasdale. One of the most familiar sights here during the season was this aged man accompanied by his wife, driving about the city, with a kindly smile and cheery greeting to those whom he knew.

John W. Teasdale was a Virginian by birth, and went to St. Louis when a boy of 10 years. For over 70 years he has been known as one of the successful business men of that city. His father was a Baptist minister, and Mr. Teasdale has been a member of the same religious denomination since childhood.

The remains were taken to St. Louis Monday night, and funeral services were held from his old home Wednesday afternoon. On account of advanced years and the fatiguing trip Mrs. Teasdale did not accompany the remains, and will spend the balance of the season here.

54

1032 CAMBRIDGE CRESCENT
NORFOLK, VIRGINIA 23508

April 29, 1976

Dear Edith Gilbert,

I know you must be receiving all kinds of
compliments for "Summer Resort Life." It will probably bring you
messages from people you have not heard from in years!!!

The pictures look fine -- and so does the
whole format. I am especially glad that something about you was
included. (I once reviewed books for the Chicago Tribune Magazine
of Books.)

Naturally, I was especially interested in the
ST material... the death of her father, what you wrote about her
on page 40, and the notes under the poem, and the letter by Mrs.
Wulfman. I am sorry that Mrs.Wulfman had not read my book, for
she would have known how passionately Vachel Lindsay was in love
with her -- and also Ernst Filsinger. There were three men, really,
in Sara's life -- those two, and John Hall Wheelock, who was a
life-long friend. (He was never romantically interested in her,
though.)

I think I understand that childhood incident
that Mrs.Wulfman remembers. Sara was an intensely private person;
one never just "dropped in" on her, not even her closest friends.
She did use that little summer house to write poetry in, and I
imagine she did not want to be interrupted at that moment. But
Mrs.Wulfman told it all as she honestly remembered it, and I can
well understand how it seemed to her as a child, too.

I can well appreciate what a job it was to
collect all this material and put it together! I have found
many interesting nuggets of information: for instance, I never
knew before how Charlevoix received its name; nor did I know
who made that remark about the five cent cigar. Nor did I really
understand the word "cottages" as used in Charlevoix before!

People you will never know, in years to come,
will thank you for preserving all this material. I feel certain
your first edition will sell out.

Again, with congratulations --

Margaret

P.S. And thank you especially for printing the acknowledgments so
carefully.

Margaret Conklin was Teasdale's friend, literary executor and
heir. Conklin died in 1984 at the age of 81.

56

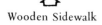

Fountain City House   Wooden Sidewalk   Argo Milling Co.
now: Weathervane Terrace   now: Weathervane I

First Steel Bridge   S.S.   Lewis Grand
City of   Opera House
Grand Rapids

Photo by Ernest Peasley, 1890.   Collection of Robert Miles.
Circa 1890

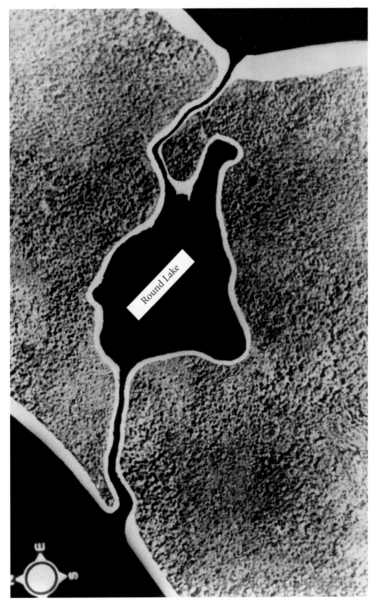

Round Lake

The original course of Pine River as it flows from Lake Michigan to Round
Lake into Lake Charlevoix

Robert Miles

THE HISTORY OF THE

Pine River
and Bridges

by
Dee Ann Rothenberger

Pine River was designated a Michigan Historic Site in commemoration of the so-called "Battle of Pine River", a scrimmage between Mormon settlers from Beaver Island and the Charlevoix "Gentile" fishermen which took place in 1853.

Pine River, said to be the shortest river in the world, joined Lake Michigan with Lake Charlevoix (formerly known as Pine Lake).

Fifty feet wide and only two feet deep, Pine River was bordered by low hanging boughs of trees on both sides of the stream. The fall of four feet of water with consequent shallows and rapids made navigation in early days almost impossible.

There was only a wooden foot bridge across the stream and horses and oxen waded across the river pulling their loaded wagons. Heavy loads were taken across on ferry-like rafts or scows.

Young school boys delighted in crossing the bridge, pulling loose planks to the opposite side and listening to the young ladies on the way to school scream for fear of being late.

In order to transport lumber and goods from and to Charlevoix, East Jordan, and Boyne City, an accessible channel had to be made and piers installed to keep the sand from washing in. This work was begun in 1869.

A notice in the local newspaper, the *Sentinel*, reads:

"Take Notice! A bee has been appointed for Thursday next. This is a matter of vital interest to every man who owns a tree on Pine Lake, and if there is not a general turnout on this day mentioned, the people deserve to live on leeks and slippery-elm for the rest of their natural existence. Turn out every man!"

The second steel bridge was built in 1901. This was the last of the swing bridges.

A dredge arrived in July of 1873 and the entire population (about 450 people) formed a reception committee. One cut of about thirty feet in width and eleven feet in depth was made through the channel.

The contract for constructing a highway pile bridge was given to Amos Fox for the sum of four hundred dollars. It was built sixteen feet above the water with a draw or lift section to let small boats through. The lift was raised and lowered by a rope running to a winch on the south shore. The bridge was operated by anyone who happened along. Now, teams of horses and oxen had a bridge to use crossing the river. A sign near the approach read:

Five dollars fine for riding or driving on this bridge faster than a walk, or for driving on more than ten head of cattle at once.

The first steel bridge, requiring the services of a tender, was officially opened on July 7, 1882. *The Fountain City* steamed slowly up the river — one thousand tons of her — amidst the blowing of whistles, ringing of bells, waving of hankerchiefs, and the shouts of the people on shore.

*   *   *

The second steel bridge, built in 1901, was operated by a large wooden bar attached to gears under the bridge. Steam power was later installed in a house near the center of the bridge.

More and more cruise ships made regular visits to the secure haven of Round Lake during the summer months. Homer D. Jones, Jr., describes his feelings as he stood by the channel during the 1920's and watched the boat traffic go by.

"My love for the sea began with the complete excitement of sailing to Charlevoix from Municipal Pier, Chicago, in the *Manitou* or *Missouri* or *Puritan.* The wardrobe trunks, the staterooms. . . the lonely lounges during storms when the crew lashed the piano and tied the furniture in groups. My spine still tingles to the deep throated blast of the *S.S. Manitou* as she drew abreast of the Coast Guard Station.[1] Like a magnificent space ship, she floated noiselessly through the channel into Round Lake with the notes of the chimes on her after-deck blending with the perfume of cooking steaks in her galley. Every chef with his head and white cap at attention out a porthole. . . passengers silently stared at the crowd on Bridge Street. . . the crowd on Bridge Street silently stared back." [2]

An amusing story is told by Irene Bond McDonnell about a summer visitor from the Belvedere Club, named Mrs. Hollingsworth, who had great presence of mind.

"I was told that when Emmett was seven years old, he and his mother (Mrs. Hollingsworth) joined the crowd watching the *Manitou* go through the channel. The ship practically filled the channel and the suction was tremendous. She had started forward movement, when Emmett fell into the channel. The whole crowd held its breath in horror — all except Mrs. Hollingsworth. She said, 'Emmett, one, two, three, kick, One, two, three, kick,' and Emmett one, two, three kicked his way to the side where someone pulled him out." [3]

*   *   *

The second steel bridge was in operation until 1947, when the present bascule bridge was built. This was named the Charlevoix Memorial Bridge in honor of the men who gave their lives during World War II.

---

1 The Coast Guard Station was located on the south entrance of the channel on Lake Michigan until 1962 when it was relocated to the north side of Round Lake near the Railroad Bridge.

2 *The Belvedere Club,* 1969. Twenty years later, Homer D. Jones, Jr., served aboard the carrier *WASP* with Commander Edward Shanahan, a Charlevoix resident and son-in-law of Dr. Armstrong.

3 *The Belvedere Club,* 1969.

The Sylvia, owned by Logan Thomson of Cincinnati, Ohio, was 191 ft. overall, steel construction, powered by two 425 Diesel engines.

In November, 1970, water whipped by an eighty mile an hour wind off Lake Michigan washed away a huge amount of soil between the bridge and the Weathervane Inn, located on the north side of the channel. It threatened to undermine the foundation of the 75-year-old landmark.[1] Subsequently, Congress appropriated $300,000 to complete a new seawall along the Weathervane property.

*   *   *

In 1975 the U.S. Corps of Engineers completed a beautification project which includes planting and landscaping a walk along the north side of the channel. A continuous concrete bench allows strollers to rest along the way and mercury vapor lights extend all the way to the pier. Future plans are under consideration to complete a similar walk on the south side of the channel.

---

1 The Weathervane Inn is located on the site of the Argo Milling Co. and many of the original hand-hewn timbers were used from the old mill.

BICENTENNIAL PROJECT:

The Charlevoix Woman's Club is spearheading the beautification of Lake Michigan Park, which extends along the south shore of the Pine River Channel. Under the master plan designed by landscape architect John Campbell, this 18-acre site will include a nature trail, new tree planting with identification markers, benches, a remodeled beach house with a new parking lot and ramps for the handicapped. Old trees along the beach will be removed and erosion control implemented. So far, $5,800 has been made available through the DNR (Department of Natural Resources) and the city is matching this sum. Work will begin in the spring of 1976.

The new Charlevoix Memorial Bridge receiving the North American cruise ship in the Pine River Channel, 1949.

Charlevoix Historical Society

Keep Michigan Beautiful, Inc. presented Edith Gilbert with an Award of Merit in 1994 for her success in persuading local, state and federal officials to replace unattractive, dangerous guard rails on the landmark Charlevoix bascule bridge, with safer and more aesthetically pleasing rails. The filigree design is based on the second steel bridge, a section of which may be seen standing in Hoffman Park on Park Ave.

The Day Culture Came To Charlevoix

by
Bernice Wexstaff
(*Grand Rapids Press*, March 27, 1966)

In the latter half of the 19th century, Charlevoix was a sprawling, lakeside village alternating between summer dust clouds, spring and autumn mud and mid-winter snows higher than a white-tailed deer's eye.

Domestic activity centered around vegetable gardens on back lots that also supported the family's milk cow, a hog or two and a flock of chickens.

There were few paying jobs available other than fishing and cutting the virgin timber in the back woods for the saws of the Charlevoix Lumber Company, which was located then as now on the northeast edge of Pine River channel.

In addition to home duties, the women worked in their church programs and sewing circles while the less serious-minded of the male population usually spent their leisure in ribald hilarity in the five saloons on main street.

This, then, was the backdrop of Charlevoix's life-stage when Esther Lewis, a strong-willed woman, and her physician husband, Levi Lewis, arrived on the scene.[1] Mrs. Lewis had the energy of a giant, and it was her decision that our backwoods settlement needed a taste of culture such as she had known in her youth in a more sophisticated section of the country.

Although Dr. Lewis was immediately caught up in a round of sick calls, his wife gave him no rest until he had agreed to build a cultural center for the community. The result was the Lewis Grand Opera House, which flourished for three decades on the south shore of Pine River channel, facing upon the crude plank boardwalk that paralleled the dusty road which was the main street of the Charlevoix business district in the not-so-good old days.

The Lewis Grand Opera House was strictly a family affair. It was designed by the Lewis family and managed by the Lewis family, which included sons, Dr. Will, attorney Rollie, and daughter Edith.

But like other so-called "opera" houses in the area, it was used for just about everything except actual operatic performances. Main floor seats were often removed for dancing or sports events, and the stage was used for public school graduation programs until a school gymnasium was built in the late 1920's.

Professional stage offerings in the old theater ran the gamut of melodrama of the era; *East Lynn, Uncle Tom's Cabin, Orphans of the Storm* were perennial tear-jerkers which brought in cash customers at the top price of 35 cents a head. Often a road-show barker would announce the following night's performance as containing a vein of humor, but the shows always proved to be the same old sob-dramas on what was known as the kerosene circuit in a day when electricity was offered in only the large metropolitan centers.

---

1 Dr. Levi Lewis, pioneer physician, located in Charlevoix in the spring of 1871. He owned the first buggy in the village. He passed away in 1920.

The interior of the plush Lewis Grand Opera House, which could accommodate 800 people "is now fully equipped with electric lights." It was built in 1881 and located on the south side of the Pine River channel on Bridge Street.
Photo by Ernest Peasley Collection of Robert Miles

The Lewis Grand Opera House was indeed an oasis of luxury and entertainment in the bleak pioneer northland. The stage curtain resembled ancient tapestry and showed the road leading to the south point. Heavy maroon velvet curtains draped the posh opera boxes on either side. Decorations were lavish in gold paint, and gilded chairs graced the exclusive box section reserved for the well-heeled elite. A balcony extended across the rear and down each side of the building while a still higher gallery in the rear offered cheaper seating for those who could afford neither box, balcony, nor main floor seats. The price of gallery seats was sometimes as low as 5 cents.

The first floor on the street level was rented to retail businesses, including a saloon for the convenience of thirsty patrons of the arts above. But the upper floor was always called the opera, perhaps to circumvent the stigma of theater in a puritanical age when the theater was considered sinful by the devout.

Shows that played the opera house were often vehicles for local talent that finally made it to Broadway. [1]

Entertainers at the turn of the century were usually accompanied by a musical aggregation and frequently staged a parade down the main street to attract attention to the evening's performance. Rita Jarvis, a professional musician and director in her own right, recalls the thrill of the mob who followed the musicians and actors up the steep steps to the ticket booth of Charlevoix's old show place.

"Talk about a thundering herd!" Rita said. "It sounded like a buffalo stampede as woodsmen in their spiked boots stomped up the narrow flight!"

Local fraternal groups often staged home talent shows to earn money for pet projects. These were usually directed by experienced directors imported from metropolitan booking agencies for the occasion. Rehearsals for these shows were long and tedious for inept amateurs, and several recall the miseries of the cold dressing rooms and unheated auditorium.

1 Charlevoix-born Forrest Wallace (junior partner in the Stoddard and Wallace Circus), as well as Agnes Miller Jarvis and her three children, Robert, Dixon and Rita, played the Opera House. Later Robert Jarvis gained fame as a blackface comedian years before blackface became taboo. Following solo performances, he gained renown as leading man in the *Gingham Girl*, which played Europe, Australia, and the United States. Still later, he promoted theater-in-the-round with its originator, St. John Terrell, and such other giants of the theatrical world as Sigmund Romburg, Oscar Hammerstein, and Richard Rodgers.

Leo Carey, father of the legendary Carey twins[1] — a two-man team almost unbeatable in football, basketball, and track — relates that the first basketball game played in Charlevoix was played in the Lewis Opera House. But, he adds, "It wasn't much of a game — nobody knew the rules very well." At one point during the game, the ball missed the target basket and sailed through an open window into Pine River below. The game had to be stopped as the team had only the one ball, which one of the substitute players retrieved from the icy waters of the channel.

Some of the youngsters who didn't have the 15-cent price of admission often climbed a telephone pole adjacent to an open window and swung themselves onto the balcony.

Sometimes Dr. Lewis had difficulty in collecting his nightly rentals from indigent actors. At this time, he would stride down the center aisle just as the performance was getting under way, and shout, "Stop the show! Stop the show! The rent hasn't been paid!" Son, Will Lewis, invariably tried to quiet his irate father as he made his way down the aisle, but the blustering old man refused to be quiet until he got money, which was usually forthcoming to avoid a mass exodus for refunds at the box office. [2]

Early in this century, the opera house was converted to a nickelodeon and then finally to a hotel called the Alhambra. In the late 40's, the Michigan Highway Department razed the building to make way for the new bascule bridge approach across the Pine River channel. All that remains now of the site is a grassy terrace sloping gently down to the channel abutment.

1 Bill and Bob Carey attended Michigan State University. During the 1951-52 season Bob was voted the best all-around athlete that had attended the University. He was also named All-American football and track star.

2 The late Clark C. Coulter, Detroit attorney, recalled that this performance far outshone the evening's entertainment.

Charlevoix Courier
Wednesday, July 14, 1920

Smith College
Tea Room Opens

WHAT THE PEOPLE ARE SAYING
ABOUT NEW VENTURE

Aunt Janie's Strawberry Tarts Have
Already Become Famous — A Place
for a Jolly Good Time

From present indications, the Smith College Tea Room, located at the corner of Petoskey Avenue and Burns Street, is making a hit among summer visitors as well as local people. Following are a few notes sent to *The Courier* for publication by those interested in the success of the new venture:

What "Aunt Janie" Thinks

"Aunt Janie" thinks there never were such kind people in the world as inhabit Charlevoix. Citizens and summer residents alike have united to help make the tea-room (corner Petoskey Avenue and Burns Street) a success. ("Aunt Janie" is the chaperone of the young Smith College girls who are managing the tea room, and her strawberry tarts are already becoming famous.)

Kind hands have helped make the rooms attractive. Miss Martha Wilson, of the Chicago Club brings gifts of fruit and flowers almost daily. Mrs. Robert Stuart presented the tea room lately with a crock of butter — a golden gift indeed these days — from "Breezy Point Farm." Others have given money, to help in expenses. With such friends success is assured.

Interior of ice cream factory on Round Lake owned by W. L. Johnson, originator of Velvet ice cream and the slogan "Charlevoix-the-Beautiful." 1905.
Charlevoix Historical Society

Saturday Nights

The tea-room will be open Saturday nights hereafter, if the patronage warrants it. Sandwiches, salads, waffles (on cool nights) — a number of good things await you there.

"Dutch Treaters"

There is in Chicago a smart little club, known as "The Dutch Treaters." All its members are society people, who rather enjoy the novelty of going to out-of-the-way restaurants, tea-shops and entertainment. At regular intervals during the winter, they dine some place together going later to the movies or some other show, each always paying his or her own way. (The club contains both men and girls.)

Why not have a "Dutch Treat Club" in Charlevoix, pledged to take Saturday night lunch at the Smith College Tea Room? You will have good food, served by college girls, a jolly, informal time, in pleasing surroundings and you'll be helping a good cause.

What Dr. Armstrong Says:

Dr. Armstrong[1] thinks the Smith College Tea Room is the nicest place in Charlevoix, and announces himself as one of its "outside boosters." Everyone takes Dr. Armstrong's word, and it can be relied on here.

Black Oil Cloth for Sale

Have you seen the tables and benches covered with black oil cloth at the tea-room? If so, you will be glad to know that there is a little of this material available there. It is the last word in artistic materials for porch-pillows, as it can be left out in the rain without injury. The best interior decorators in Chicago are using quantities of this now, and it is hard to get.

1 Dr. Robert Bruce Armstrong, graduate of the University of Michigan, began his Charlevoix practice in 1894 and remained in this community until his death in 1940. He was known and loved as the typical country doctor who arrived by horse and buggy in a blinding snow storm and operated on the kitchen table when necessary. He was mayor of Charlevoix in 1907.

Every summer in July Charlevoix celebrates its Venetian Festival with gaily decorated boats and massive fireworks. Thousands of visitors sit in the park, or enjoy the view from their cottages or anchored yachts in Round Lake.

Charlevoix Historical Society

Charlevoix Courier, Front Page, July 2, 1913

INTERNATIONAL

Flying Boats
Race Here

July 11-12

The greatest event in the history of aviation in America is the endurance test for flying boats which is being pulled off in the race from Chicago to Detroit around the shore of the lakes. . . Among the Chicago aviators to enter is Harold McCormick, son-in-law of John D. Rockefeller, who will be a passenger in his own boat.

Charlevoix has been designated as a night control and all contestants will land in Round Lake . . . and the next day make their start for Mackinac . . . this giving summer visitors to Charlevoix an unexampled opportunity to see the boats at close range and witness their various maneuvers in flying in the air, on the water, and rising and alighting.

Capt. Allie Moore — One of the great sailors of his time and expert rope splicer. Remembered for his sailing feat when he would bring in a two-masted 60-ft. sailing schooner through the channel under full sail, if the wind was right. (He also claimed the title of World Champion Roller Skater and during a European tour skated before the King and Queen of England.) He was sailing instructor at the Belvedere Club during the summer. He built his own sailboat. The small replica is now located on the channel near the Weathervane Inn. From 1934 to 1941, he was the Captain on the *Sylvia G.* a 65-ft. luxury yacht, powered by a twin screw diesel engine, and owned by Samuel T. Gilbert, Detroit.

THE BROODING, ICY WINTER
OF NORTHERN MICHIGAN, AS FOUND IN

Mark Smith's Odd Book

by
Edith Gilbert
(*Detroit Free Press*, October 15, 1967)

Anyone interested in one-upmanship might score with the question: "What author has something in common with Hemingway, Faulkner, and Camus?" Chances are pretty slim that anyone will come up with the correct answer — Mark Smith.

According to *The New York Times*, Smith's book, *The Middleman*, published by Little, Brown & Co. is one of the best existential novels yet written in the United States.

The reviewer claims that Smith's sardonic and absurd humor is reminiscent of Faulkner, but that the theme of his book is closer to Camus.

That's pretty heady stuff for a young writer of 32 born in a town as small as Charlevoix, Michigan (Population 2,700).

Charlevoix, where Smith's grandparents' boarding house[1] overlooked Lake Michigan in the heart of early Hemingway country, is the setting for *The Middleman*.

---

1 Presently the site of the Dunes Condominiums.

"Much of the original idea of the novel came from stories of Charlevoix I heard told by my family — that and those wonderful, mysterious remembrances of a very young childhood."

In World War II, when Smith was only about eight and his parents were divorced, he moved to Battle Creek and Grant, Michigan, his mother's family home, returning to Charlevoix for brief visits during his early 20's. He hasn't been back since, and much of the novel is based on his childhood memories.

What memories they were!

"The summer way of life as I knew it was to go out with the limousines and chauffeurs, the maids and cooks and nurses, who on a sunny day would paint the streets of the town with the colors of their uniforms," he says.

The photo taken in 1950 is of Miss Evans and John Wineman of Detroit. This was the end of the era of baby nurses and the beginning of the baby sitter.

However, Smith's fantastic imagination unfolds not in the streets but in the rambling hallucinations of narrator Walter Wold, who becomes obsessed by a piece of chalk. Though the story covers only one day, flashbacks move the story back and forth through vast stretches of time.

The New York Times accused Smith of portraying the residents of Charlevoix in an unflattering light. Smith denies he did this intentionally.

"About the only biographical element in the story is about a father and his sons daydreaming about establishing a resort on Fisherman's Island, which was true of my grandfather and his sons," he says.

"This very dream and what it did to the family, and especially to the imaginary character of Walter, was what compelled me to write the book."

"If anyone in Charlevoix is going to play the game of guessing who is who in the book, well, I can't stop them. . ." Indeed you can't. Nor what's located where, either — Fisherman's Island, for instance. The island, a favorite picnic area in Lake Michigan, is misplaced in Smith's book. The persistent daydreams of the Wold family are to develop Fisherman's Island into an ultra-exclusive resort. You can't see Fisherman's Island from the Smith-Wold boarding house as in the story, and one local reviewer has been quick to point this out. Here's the reason: Smith erroneously recalled from childhood days that the island was in Lake Charlevoix, and whimsically relocated the island in Lake Michigan. As it turns out, one can almost see it from the old boarding house on Michigan Avenue. [1]

---

1 One can actually see South Point though. A family story often told goes like this: It was always a rush getting places ready for summer visitors, and Grandpa George Smith was one to procrastinate. One June day his wife Minnie impatiently said, "George, you'll be painting the toilet seat when the *Manitou* comes 'round the point!"

In 1945 Smith moved to Maywood, Illinois, and a year or so later he went to Chicago where he attended Taft High School. He entered Western Michigan University in Kalamazoo, transferred to Wright Junior College in Chicago, then to the University of Chicago, and graduated from Northwestern.

Smith's 20th summer was spent as a sailor on the Great Lakes, but it was not the lusty, carefree time he'd anticipated. He was seriously injured in Calcite on Lake Huron when he was crushed between his ship and the dock. He spent a long time in the Marine Hospital in Detroit waiting for his injuries, which included a broken pelvis, to heal.

Despite this, Smith has fond memories of Michigan.

"When I was living in Chicago, whenever the weather was good and the fancy struck, I would hop into the car and drive to Michigan," he says. "My favorite places in Michigan are the Kewaunee Peninsula and any of the waterfalls in the Upper Peninsula."

"In the Lower Peninsula, my favorite spots are, of course, the Charlevoix — Harbor Springs — Petoskey area and the Leelanau Peninsula and the dunes at Mears — if I can get there about 5 in the morning when tourists aren't scrambling over the hills and I can feel like I am Lawrence of Arabia."

"Then there's that Polish tavern in Cross Village, which was worth the long drive up from Chicago just to drink a beer there, and is no doubt worth the long trip from New Hampshire too."

New Hampshire is where Smith now lives with his wife and three daughters. He teaches English and creative writing at the University of New Hampshire.

However, Smith still considers himself a Midwesterner as far as his writing is concerned. His first two books have both used Midwestern settings, with the first one, *Toyland*, being clearly related to *The Middleman*. [1]

Anyone who has ever rocked on a summer-cottage porch in Charlevoix will probably be interested in knowing that the composite of the Wold boardinghouse of Smith's fearful imagination still stand on Michigan Avenue as two large white frame three-story "cottages." One was built in 1917 by David May, the founder of May Department Stores, and the other by his brother-in-law, Col. Beaumont.

Either house is large enough to accommodate the sizable basement where the insane Walter Wold builds his own miniature Charlevoix, complete with electric trains, cardboard houses, and predictable plastic people.

Speaking of people, plastic and otherwise, Smith says, "There are certain truths in the characters of the novel that I feel are especially applicable to Charlevoixans, and yet, if the writing is valid, the same truths, in different degrees, are applicable to anyone else living anywhere in America."

☆☆☆

Mark Smith, author of *The Middleman* (Little, Brown & Co., 1967) teaches English and creative writing at the University of New Hampshire, where he lives with his wife and three daughters.

His latest book is called *The Detective*, (Knopf, 1974) and the locale is Chicago.

Childhood Daydreams from the 20's

The Smiths' original summer boarding house and family winter residence on Nichols Street, where Mark Smith lived as a boy. It did not seem so large and mysterious to the man, so he used the houses on Michigan Avenue.

Photo by Robert Miles

These two "summer cottages" on Michigan Ave. were built in 1917 by David May, founder of the May Company, and his brother-in-law, Louis D. Beaumont (formerly Schoenberg). Both cottages are the composite of the Wold boarding house as described by Mark Smith in his unusual novel *The Middleman*.

Photo taken in 1967 by Robert Miles

This picture was taken in the spring of 1967, when the house was shuttered and before present renovations. The property adjoins "The Wilds" and here is where the sidewalk ends.

Photo taken in 1967 by Robert Miles

No Smoking Award

"Mt. McSaube on Lake Michigan beach, about a mile north of the channel entrance, is one of the highest dunes on the east shore of the lake and it was the goal of one of our favorite boy gang hikes. We would slowly climb the sand path (it went straight up on the east slope) going two steps up and sliding back one-and-a-half steps. When we finally reached the top, we climbed the small wooden look-out tower. On a clear day, the view was wonderful — Beaver Island to the west and Boyne City to the east.

"One night in 1913 about a dozen of us hiked to the sandy beach on the west side of Mt. McSaube for an over-night camp-out. We took blankets, a skillet and eggs. We nearly froze as the cool lake fog rolled in all night, and when the sea gulls started flying and squawking in the pre-day light mist, we were cold and sleepy and, thinking it must be mid-morning, decided to go home to our beds. As we trudged through town a clock in a store window on Bridge Street showed it was only 4:55 a.m. When we reached our cottages, we had to waken our parents to get inside. In those days youngsters never had watches. Watches were received as 'rewards' for attaining the age of eighteen or twenty-one years without smoking."[1]

1 Joe Bohrer, in *The Belvedere Club*, 1969.

The End of an Era

This photograph was taken in 1977, in front of one of the oldest cottages — 405 Michigan Avenue. It pictures uniformed staff from St. Louis and Chicago chatting in the sunlight on the front lawn during a break.

HIGH-ROLLING AT CHARLEVOIX'S

Old Colonial Club

by
Edith Gilbert

(*Detroit Free Press*, February 3, 1974)

I almost wish they wouldn't tear the old place down now, but of course that's impossible. The Colonial Club has been condemned for years. The roof's gone, windows smashed, one of the pillars by the front entrance has disappeared leaving a gaping hole like a missing tooth in a craggy, weatherbeaten face. In the summer, tall weeds clutch the peeling dirty white siding, trying like everything to protect the structure from questioning tourists' eyes. It all reminds me of an old Indian graveyard a few miles away, where tilted tombstones are also matted with weeds. These graves are not neglected, mind you! They appear unkept because the Indians believe their ancestors should be left to rest in peace. Literally.

And I kind of feel the same way about this hopeless old wreck of a building. Let the sagging, disheveled Colonial Club also rest in peace, untouched by the hot breath of the bulldozers, the cranes, and the cement mixers that are about to burrow, spit, and chew the old place into oblivion.

Original 7-bedroom home of Fred J. Meech, a florist, built 1895. Picture shows home after Mr. Koch remodeled it and before the fire.

In its glory, the Colonial Club, or Koch's (pronounced Cook's), was quite a gambling place! (The cogniscenti say there was only one other place like it and that was Bradley's in Palm Beach, Florida, where the elite went during the 20's and 30's.) Even as the building stands today, it still has an aura of majesty about it — a majesty that attracted one of our local artists to spend several days sketching the entrance in such a delightful way that the sun hits the pillared portico just so, framing it between two tall iron gates standing a lonely sentinel to the weeds.

But I recall an earlier sentinel, the doorman, Frank Poole, who knew everyone. He knew who was allowed in and who was not. Summer people for the most part (if they were dressed properly in a coat and tie) were allowed in. Year 'round Charlevoix people or "townies" were kept out. All that is, except the local doctors and banker. But even they were only allowed to dance and dine in Mr. Gatti's fabulous restaurant and not to gamble in the adjoining green carpeted room which was Mr. Koch's private domain. (John Koch owned the Club and gave the restaurant concession to O. Gatti.)

From the moment a guest drove his car up to the front entrance, he felt pampered. His car was parked for him when he arrived and later returned to him when he was ready to leave — without a car check, even on a Saturday night when there were as many as 150 cars!

Parking attendants were paid only $30 a week but made as much as $200 a week in tips. Those were the days before unemployment insurance and some families lived all winter on what Dad earned during those two summer months. There's a story that still is making the rounds locally about a skin-flint resorter who fostered such resentment that one of the attendants used to relieve himself in the fellow's gas tank every Saturday night !

As one entered the club, there was a huge bouquet of fresh red roses in the square entrance hall. To the right was the ladies' coat room with an attendant. Beyond there was the card room. Straight ahead was the gambling room, and to the left of the hall was the dining room with a dance floor in the center. Upstairs on the second and third floor were cell-like accommodations for the waiters and croupiers brought from Florida.

The first time I was taken to Koch's was in 1940. I was told that Ernest Hemingway was one of the notables who visited the place. Constance Cappel Montgomery describes an incident in her book *Hemingway in Michigan*:

"During the summer of 1920, Hemingway often played tennis with Ted Brumback, Bill Smith and Dr. Charles in Charlevoix. On August 9th of that summer in a letter to Edith Quinlan, he described his experience at a gambling place named Cooks, in the town of Charlevoix. He had just been "kicked out" of his family's summer cottage and was thinking about finding work at the cement plant in Petoskey, until the night he played roulette until two in the morning. Hemingway started with six dollars and had won fifty-nine when the group he was with wanted to go home. He wrote that he quit with his profit and was saved from the cement plant."

Through these gates walked "the beautiful people" of the 30's. No cameras were allowed on the premises — it was all too hush-hush!
Photo by Dan Perszyk for the *Detroit Free Press*, 1974.

I tried to look at the group around me through his eyes. God, they were rich! And they lived like royalty in their 30-room "cottages" staffed with uniformed servants. Some of the ladies could entertain a hundred people in great style and with ease, but they couldn't find their way to the kitchen on cook's night out. Instead, they headed for Koch's, and there they'd sit playing 10 cent chips, which women were allowed to do. One of the ladies, an ardent fisherwoman I recall, gleefully exchanged angling tips with the croupier between turns of the wheel.

But for the most part, the group was made up of "Merchant Princes" whose power lay in their vast holdings of steel, leather, paper, cereal, cotton, tobacco and sugar — all listed alphabetically on the big board of the New York Stock Exchange. Their factories and offices were located in the smoky cities of the Midwest for the most part, Chicago, St. Louis, Detroit, Cincinnati — an easy overnight trip by train to the heavenly cool summer air of Charlevoix in Northern Michigan.

And so they came north, year after year, with their entourages, nodding to each other on the dance floor, smiling at each other in the dining room, exchanging gossip in the men's room and whispering introductions in the gambling room where no drinks were served. Why, you couldn't even take a Coke in there with you! There was no bar at Koch's either, a holdover, no doubt, from Prohibition days when everyone brought his own bottle, purchased surreptitiously from one's own favorite bootlegger and delivered home after midnight or in the wee hours of the morning. Drinks were served only in the dining room during the entire 27 years of the Club's existence.

The memorable night the excitement started was a usual Thursday in August. The casino was crowded because it was the height of the season and Thursday was traditionally cook's night out. There were several private parties in the dining room. Mr. Gatti was in rare form — all five feet two of him. He used to say, "There's no use for me to retire — I never learned how to play!" But he knew how to run a fine restaurant! Simultaneously he could order a waiter to open a window or remove an extra chair at a table while he answered the telephone and took reservations, greeted important guests, sent directions to the French chef in the kitchen, and give his wife, the cashier, instructions in Italian. But most of all he could produce a meal that still brings a deep sigh to many a staunch admirer. There were the *hors d'ouevres* carts filled with antipasto. There were Chicken Cacciatore and Veal Scallopini and fresh lobsters brought in every Friday night. There were filet strips with Bernaise sauce and salad dressing made with Italian olive oil and fresh farm vegetables. Then for dessert, the pastry carts were wheeled around again by Gatti's son "Little" Joe; choices of fresh fruit pies and tarts, glazed with red currant jelly, bordered with chopped nuts, or fresh coconut cake or Boston cream cake, eclairs, napoleons; or if this didn't suit, one could order spumoni ice cream or baked Alaska. None of this "institutional" restaurant glop! It was all made from scratch.

"I don't mind when my customers complain about the prices — but I do mind when they complain about the food!" he used to say. Actually, the privilege of complaint rightfully belonged more to Gatti than to his privileged customers. Their demands were endless.

"Your steak is too well done? Never mind, we'll get you another one!"

"You can't eat sweets? How about half a grapefruit instead!"

"The champagne is flat? We're so sorry! Here's another bottle."

When a group of resort teenagers dropped in during the week, he would good-naturedly serve them Cokes, but on a Saturday night, his patience exhausted, he would point his finger to the door and cry, "OUT!"

After dinner, guests danced, played cards, or strolled into the gambling room. During Mr. Koch's reign there were only roulette tables, but in my time, Mr. Koch had already sold his interest to an associate, Marsh Meek, and a crap table was installed. My husband enjoyed playing a little roulette occasionally, but I preferred the action at the crap table. My usual routine was to buy $10 worth of chips and roll the dice until I either doubled my money or lost it all. On this particular Thursday, the craps table was surrounded by a lively group of men from Memphis and St. Louis. They were dressed in white lightweight summer suits and dark shirts with white ties, which was the fashion that year. In this game the limit was $200 on the line. There were exceptions because every person had his own color chip, and the management could establish any limit on these. One could make place bets as well as line bets and bet behind the line. I waited my turn and finally the croupier noticed me and gave me my usual little stack of chips. When he finally handed me the dice, I made passes and made my points, again and again and again. A hush fell around the table and I could see stacks of chips sliding back and forth across the green felt. In the meantime, I was betting one chip at a time! Another pass and another until I made 13 passes before I lost the dice. I won $13, but my gambling companions walked away with $7,000 each! From then on I was known publicly as the girl with the golden arm, but privately, I think of myself as the girl with the cotton head! I didn't know how to shoot craps then, nor do I now.

This I do know. There was and still is a strong conviction among those who patronized the Colonial Club that this was the only "honest" gambling house in the country.

"And why not?" Koch used to say. "The margin at the roulette wheel is always in favor of the house by four percent, 52 percent for the house and 48 percent for the players."

The secret of his success was two-fold. First, he catered to his clientele; and second, he knew exactly whom to pay off and how much, because in 27 years he was never raided! The club was open every day during the summer. On Sunday there was no drinking or gambling, and families used to bring their children for dinner. The card room, with its gold brocade walls, was open for private bridge games and people went home early. The rest of the week, hours varied. When everyone went home, it was closing time, and that could be at daybreak. Ladies who enjoyed gambling would often play in the afternoons, or if someone felt like staying late at night, the watchman would escort her home safely.

"Townies" had mixed feelings about the Colonial Club.

On the one hand, they were disappointed that gambling and liquor laws were not enforced, but on the other hand, they were pleased that it attracted such a wealthy clientele to the area — people who spent money in town, which meant jobs. Rumor has it that even one of Michigan's Governors dropped by and when he admired a copper sailing ship, John Koch gave it to him for his office in Lansing. Koch had a great personality and sense of humor, reinforced no doubt by his daily fifth of Whitehorse. At the end of the season, after Labor Day, Koch made an annual trip down-state to pay off the right people, which netted him among other benefits the privilege of owning license number 2 on his car. (The Governor had number 1.) When the Club was finally raided during Mr. Meek's ownership, Koch remarked, "Meek didn't put out enough or didn't put it in the right place!"

There were other dangers in running a gambling club besides being raided. There was the time one of the guests stole money from Koch's desk in his private office, and then there was the extraordinary event I saw with my own eyes. I was standing by the roulette table nearest the entrance watching my husband Julius play, eager to tell him of my fabulous thirteen passes, when all of a sudden Meek swooped down on a lady standing beside me. She wore a long black evening dress and carried a black satin clutch bag tucked under her elbow. In firm, quiet tones he said, "Come with me", and whisked her reluctantly away. At the same moment another croupier pounced on a man dressed in black tie seated at the roulette table and led him sputtering out of the room, too. Without missing a beat, another croupier placed himself behind the wheel, spun it and said, "Ladies and gentlemen, place your bets."

We were indignant! Nothing like this had ever happened before! Who were these people who were so rudely jostled and swept out of the room? Soon Meek returned and softly explained. The lady had a bent clothes hanger protruding from the fold of her evening bag. She'd lean forward, oh, ever so slightly, and touch the ball as it rolled around and around the wheel in such a way that it would drop into a certain section. Her companion was placing his chips on the same numbers within that section on the board. They thought they had a sure system to cheat the house, but Meek became suspicious of the couple from the moment they walked into the Club. Why? Because it was Thursday night, and the "regulars" dressed in evening clothes only on Fridays and Saturdays! Never on Thursday. Ah, such are the slips that disasters are made of —

In spite of Meek's alertness on this occasion, it was the beginning of the end for the Colonial Club. A new governor, Kim Sigler, declared war on all gambling in Michigan, which covered slot machines as well as the few resort gambling houses left in northern Michigan.

The posh Colonial Club, crumbling and almost forgotten as time passes by.
Photo by Dan Perszyk for the *Detroit Free Press*, 1974.

Locally it also became more and more difficult to hide the knowledge that gambling existed in Charlevoix, Harbor Springs, and Mackinac Island. In nearby Petoskey, at a public meeting of the Liquor Control Commission, an irate bar owner objected that a local inspector bitched about there not being a drain in the men's toilet at his place.

"Ye gods," he cried, "at Koch's he's got to walk past four roulette tables and a craps table to get to the men's toilet!" Which broke up that meeting in a hurry!

In September, 1947, on what the summer people called "get away night," a few resorters made their reservations at the club. One of the guests recalls "dropping $2,500 before dinner." A little while later, while eating dinner, the State Police walked in and "found gambling equipment hidden behind a secret mirror," or so the newspapers said. Troopers carried out all the gambling equipment through the front door, past the iron fence that surrounded the club, and loaded it on a truck.[1] It was one of the quietest raids in history. The people in the dining room kept right on eating— "What else could one do?"

The Governor was disturbed by reports that the recent raids by the two State agencies on gambling places in the Charlevoix-Harbor Springs area were only "token raids" because they came in the final week of the resort season, although authorities had reports that gambling had existed since late June.

"I want to find out if someone pulled a fast one," Governor Sigler was quoted as saying in the papers.

The Liquor Commissioner said it had occurred to him that it was "strange" that his own investigators and the State Police "took so long" to close the gambling clubs.

Both Marsh Meek, who owned the equipment, and Oreste Gatti, who owned the liquor license, were bound over to circuit court, according to the papers. And poor Mr. Gatti subsequently broke out with a bad case of the virus disease, shingles.

---

1 Years later, Jack Uhrick recalls "exploring" inside the club during his high school days with friends. They found mountains of gaming equipment still piled high behind this mirror.

With gambling gone, there was no way to run a profitable two-month restaurant operation as Gatti had done for so many years. Not without a liquor license.

Did it hurt the town when Koch's was closed? Temporarily, yes, but shortly thereafter, the black tie gamblers were replaced by skiers in stretch pants. To accommodate the new year-round resorters, numerous condominiums were built. Now, plans are finally underway to tear down the old Colonial Club and build much needed apartments.

For old times' sake, I hope they will name them Colonial Club Apartments !

The leaky structure was finally torn down during the summer of '74, much to everyone's relief.

Photo by Dan Perszyk for the *Detroit Free Press*, 1974.

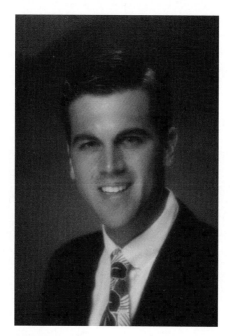

Pat McKeown Jr.

The Changing Face of Charlevoix

by
Pat McKeown Jr.

As we move closer to the year 2000, we begin to see the face of Charlevoix the Beautiful rapidly changing. On the up side, the Charlevoix Historical Society has acquired both the Harsha House on State Street, and the old Railroad Depot on Lake Charlevoix. The Harsha House was restored to its original Queen Anne grandeur during the mid-1980's, and the familiar depot is currently awaiting funding before undergoing a major restoration.

On the minus side, some historical landmarks, which define the very essence of our quaint little town, have been slowly stripped away or are threatened. Unless some faithful Charlevoix supporters step up to the plate and save the old water tower, it will probably come crashing down sometime in the future. In the mid-1980's we lost the historic Pere Marquette railroad swing bridge and in 1994 we said goodbye to both the Bellinger Marina on Round Lake and the familiar Parkside Restaurant.

It was on Labor Day that the Parkside served its last meal, closed its doors, and sold off all its contents. Both Charlevoix residents and tourists, lamented the fact that this popular meeting place was going out of business for good. It was time for the beloved owners, Leo and Gladys Markel, to retire to Florida.

While dining during the final week of service at the Parkside, I also savored, along with the whitefish and banana bread, the many years of happy memories this little restaurant provided. Chatting with Leo, he told me how pleased he was to hear that his restaurant would be remembered in this updated version of *Summer Resort Life*. It lifted his spirits to know that the Parkside would not be forgotten and would remain a small part of this town's nostalgic past. In gratitude he gave me an original Bob Miles photograph, one that had been hanging on the wall since he bought the place in 1978, and who knows how much longer before that.

In its heyday, the Parkside employed around 45 Charlevoix youths each summer — from Memorial Day to Labor Day. Multiply this over eighteen years of operations, that results in an amazing number of kids that have literally grown up here. At one time, there were a set of triplets and two sets of twins working simultaneously in the restaurant as cooks, waiters, and bussers, which created the illusion that caused many patrons to believe they were seeing double, or even triple!

Leo estimated that on a busy summer day, 800 meals were served, and during the course of a week, over 2,000 pounds of whitefish was cooked in the Parkside kitchen.

The final weeks at the Parkside were difficult for the Markels, but this happy little building will always hold fond "MMMM....what a place" memories for many people.

The Parkside Restaurant after it closed in 1994.

Photo by Pat McKeown Jr.

Bellinger Marina
Time Sails On

While the white, corner building that housed the Parkside Restaurant is still standing, another familiar Charlevoix landmark, the Bellinger Marina, was torn down in the fall of 1994. The large, white structure with the hunter green trim was easily the most recognizable site on the south shore of Round Lake.

The marina was the subject of the popular watercolor print by Kathleen Chaney Fritz, a contemporary Michigan artist. Her work also commemorates the prestigious Waterfront Art Fair and currently appears on the front cover of *Summer Resort Life*.

Bellinger's began as a fishery in the 1920's, and was called Booth's Fisheries. In 1950, James Bellinger bought the business and converted it into a marina, where they sold gas, and stored and repaired boats. Until its demolition, Bellinger's was the hub of boating activity on Round Lake. The marina was sold to one of the Winn brothers, who started the Four Winns boat company. Thus, one might say, the bulldozed site still clings by a thread to the nautical history of the original property. Currently it is awaiting the construction of two new residences for the Winns brothers.

Bellinger Marina two days before it was demolished.

Photo by Pat McKeown, Jr.

Left to right standing: James Bellinger, Jerry Simpson, Joe Arvilla. Kneeling: Man on left unknown, Ted Shupek, Johnny Clauson, Harold Behnedsen.

Charlevoix Historical Society

THE CHARLEVOIX SONG
by
The Charlevoices

On a related note to the saga of the Bellinger Marina, we should add that Alice Bellinger, the sister-in-law of James Bellinger, was one of a trio called "Charlevoices". This group of three ladies, including Esther Hawley and Mildred Webster, enjoyed singing with the popular (SPEBSQSA) Barber Shop Quartet singers in the area. They often sang at various parties and events during the thirties and the forties. By far, their most popular tune was "The Charlevoix Song", which was sung to the tune of the old Irish ballad "Little Bit of Heaven."

Sentimentalists have adopted this song and it is now occasionally sung at weddings and funerals. Although the author has since long been forgotten, the words go like this:

"This little bit of heaven
Mixed with land and lake and sky.

It nestles in the valleys
With Lake Michigan close by

And when the angels found it
Oh, it looked so sweet and fair

They said, 'Suppose we leave it
For it looks so peaceful there!'

So they sprinkled it with birches
Just to make the pine trees grow

O'er all the land you'll find them
No matter where you go

Then, they dotted it with blue lakes
While the angels sang for joy

And when they had it finished
Sure, they called it 'Charlevoix.'"

CHARLEVOIX HISTORICAL SOCIETY

The Harsha House
and the Railroad Depot

Since the Charlevoix Historical Society was reactivated by Ralph S. Hamilton in 1972, members have made significant strides to help preserve not only treasured memorabilia, but also two important buildings.

The Harsha House, which is one of the oldest homes in Charlevoix, is located at 103 State Street. It was built in 1891 for Horace Harsha, a local businessman and civic leader. His daughter, Anne, donated the property to the Historical Society in 1978. Since then it has been carefully restored to reflect the Victorian 90's. It now serves as headquarters for the society. The building houses archives consisting of letters and photographs, all carefully catalogued. The museum displays many artifacts reflecting the fishing, maritime, railroad and lumbering industries. In the summer it is open to the public daily from one to four o'clock and the rest of the year it is open on Saturdays. The society publishes a newsletter and has regular meetings throughout the year.

A more recent acquisition is the old Railroad Depot, located at Depot Beach on Lake Charlevoix, next to the Chicago Club.

The land that the Depot stands on was originally known as the Dixon Terrace Farm. In the late 1880's, the farm was parceled off and a piece of the property was purchased by the Chicago & Western Michigan Railroad, which later merged with two other railroads and became the Pere Marquette Railroad. Here both the Depot and the Inn Hotel were built. Another large section was purchased by the Chicago Club, on which they built homes and an eighteen-hole golf course. The golf course was later sold to the city of Charlevoix for one dollar, and it was divided into the present Industrial Park, leaving only a nine-hole municipal golf course.

The first train rolled into Charlevoix on June 26, 1892 and the "Inn Depot," as it was called in that day, serviced both freight and passengers. The Depot was a Victorian white structure, trimmed in green with a black roof. A white picket fence and carefully laid out brickwork surrounded the building. From this area, horse-drawn rigs would shuttle passengers into town.

Between the Depot and Lake Charlevoix was a broad lawn where passengers could relax on a warm summer day. White stone walkways stretched down to the beach and manicured shrubbery was everywhere. There was even a fountain and a pond where passengers could rest on benches. For over forty years, the word "Charlevoix" was spelled out on this wide lawn in big letters made up of small variegated rocks. Though now overgrown and unattended, some of the shrubs and trees still grow here. If you look closely, you can still identify the white pathways that led across the lawn.

Currently fundraising efforts are underway to restore the Depot to its original grandeur. Jim Annis, a popular Charlevoix artist, better known for his paintings of historical Chicago landmarks such as Wrigley Field, has done a charming painting of the Depot, which is available as a print from the Historical Society. Hopefully enough money will be raised in the future to not only restore the structure, but also the Depot grounds.

The Resort Special is leaving the Depot. A 1937 Pierce Arrow is shown in the picture.

Acrylic by Jim Annis

THE END OF THE RAILROAD

Soon after World War II, when people could again travel world wide, during the late forties and early fifties, the summer resort industry in Charlevoix visibly declined. The Resort Special passenger train was only running once a week now. In 1958 it was discontinued completely and the last passenger train passed through Charlevoix in 1962.

No longer did business and professional men from Chicago, Detroit, Cincinnati, and St. Louis join their vacationing families up north on the weekends. This was the end of the convenient overnight train travel. Gone were the friendly card games in the club car, congenial dinners in the fancy dining car, and even some romantic, overnight rendez-vous in the private sleeping compartments. Gone was the pampered service by smiling, uniformed porters. For the next twenty years, the railroad was only used for freight, primarily servicing the Medusa Cement plant. In 1982 the last freight train ran past the fabled Depot, and a couple of years later, nearly all the tracks were removed, along with the familiar railroad swing bridge at the mouth of Round Lake.

THE INN HOTEL

The Inn Hotel had a short, but interesting existence in Charlevoix. When conceived by the visionaries of the Chicago & Western Michigan Railroad,[1] the hotel was planned to be one of the premier establishments in the west, only second to the posh Grant Hotel on Mackinaw Island. The plan was to cash in on the growing summer resort market in Northern Michigan and to augment the lucrative business of transporting lumber. Construction of the Inn began in 1896, but immediately was met with tragedy. The builders rushed to begin plastering the upper levels of the structure, before all of the lower structural work was completed. The owners wanted to open for business as soon as possible, but 60-mile-an-hour cyclone winds blew off the lake one October day, causing the whole hotel to collapse. Records indicate that two men died, several more were injured and a team of horses was buried alive.

By 1898, after the wreckage was removed, the Inn Hotel was finally completed. It had accommodations for 500 guests and it was said to be the finest place to stay in the country. The facilities were the latest any hotel had to offer. Each room had running water and all mattresses were stuffed with hair. The dining room could easily seat 500 people at one time with a staff of up to 150 people operating the hotel. There was also an attached casino for private parties.

A separate building, called a Natatorium, housed a swimming pool. It was located between the railroad tracks and Lake Charlevoix (formerly called Pine Lake). The pool was 30 x 100 feet and the water was circulated from Lake Charlevoix. The building was two stories high with a gallery on the second floor. The swimming instructor would stand here and teach youngsters to swim, by attaching a line around the student's waist. According to the late Benona Bartlett Kohler, who had a summer job during high school at the Natatorium, bath attendants were available to issue woolen swimming suits to the bathers. Her son, Bud, says it makes him itch to even think about the woolen trunks he wore in those days.

The summer of 1940 was the last season of the Inn's operation. By the fall of 1941, the contents of this lovely, but out-dated wooden hotel were auctioned off and the building was demolished. Driving down Dixon Avenue today, one can still see the former magnificence of the Hotel by the imposing, original stone stairway that led up to the Hotel from the Depot, by the old street lamps and the half circle drive on Mercer Blvd.

1 In 1900 the Chicago & Western Michigan Railroad merged with two other railroads to form the Pere Marquette Railroad.

THE INN
"Charlevoix-the-Beautiful"
MICHIGAN

LUNCHEON

Pineapple Juice

Puree of Yellow Split Pea Soup   Consomme en Tasse
Jellied Bouillon

Sweet Mixed Pickles   Watermelon Pickles

Fried Fillet of Sole, Tartar Sauce
Long Branch Potatoes

Baked Chicken Pie, Individual
Breaded Veal Cutlet, Tomato Sauce
Toasted, Open Club Sandwich, Inn Style

Roast Loin of Fresh Pork, Apple Sauce

Mashed Potatoes   Saute Potatoes
Steamed Hominy
Succotash   Green Beans

Cold—Ham   Ox Tongue
Lamb   Chicken   Bologna   Kippered Herring
Salami   Sardines

Hearts of Lettuce   Sliced Tomatoes   Asparagus Salad
French, Mayonnaise, Roquefort, Russian and Thousand Island Dressing

Hot Rolls

Cocoanut Custard Pie   Sherbet
Lemon Jello, Whipped Cream   Cookies
Sliced Peaches   Sliced Watermelon   Sliced Bananas
Preserved—Pears, Pineapple, Apricots, Peaches, Apple Sauce
Camembert, Edam, American, Swiss, Cream Cheese
Saltines
Tea   Cocoa   Coffee   Buttermilk   Milk
Kaffee Hag, Sanka or Postum

July 12, 1939

The Inn Hotel as it appeared in the 1930's.

Robert Miles Photo

In 1896 the railroad built the fashionable Inn on Lake Charlevoix. It was said to be "one of the finest summer hotels in the nation." The great dining room could seat well over 500 people.

Northern Michigan State Champion golfer, Julius Gilbert, played an exhibition round for the opening of the Bay View Country Club in 1919.

A GOLF POEM

Courses were scarce and golfers few
In the halcyon days of ninety-two.
The greens were slow, the fairways dry.
The gentleman golfer wore a tie.
The lady golfer wore a hat...
It was a must, and that was that.
The caddies were young, the bags were light,
Eight clubs or less would be just right.
Wood shafted clubs, each name its own;
The numbered club as yet unknown.
The driver, midiron, spoon and brassie,
The niblick, putter, cleek and mashie.

The game's not changed much, overall;
A bag of clubs and a little ball.

From Bob Miles' *Charlevoix*

Banking in Charlevoix
Always Friendly Rivals

The town of Charlevoix received its charter in 1879, and by 1882 the first bank was established. The corner of Bridge Street and Park Avenue (currently the site of Vacation Properties) was the place The Bank of Charlevoix chose to begin operations. It was a private bank that was owned by two men named Reynolds and Brown. Mr. W. P. Brown was a friend of Michigan's governor, J. W. Begole, at the time. In a lavish celebration of the first observance of Labor Day in the State of Michigan, the governor came to Charlevoix for a parade down Bridge Street.

In 1885, The Bank of Charlevoix moved to the corner of Bridge and Clinton Street, the latter street was known at this time as Hoop Skirt Alley. The bank operated out of this building which is still used by Murdick's Fudge today.

Across the street, at the site now occupied by Carey's Boot Shop, the Charlevoix Savings Bank opened its doors in 1884. Assets of only $33,000 were all it took to launch the completion. It was reorganized in 1899 and became the Charlevoix County State Bank. The first bank president, John Nichols, along with Archie Butters and Robert Bridge, secured the site at the corner of Bridge and Clinton, right opposite the Bank of Charlevoix, and built the red brick structure still used today. This building was completed in 1905 and was the hub of downtown commerce. In addition to the bank on the ground floor, the building was home to the J. L. Crane dry-goods store, offices on the second floor, and a dance hall and lodge rooms on the third floor.

In February, 1924, tragedy hit the Charlevoix County State Bank. In one of the worst fires in Charlevoix history, the bank was destroyed. Reportedly, the temperature was minus 22 degrees that winter day, and nothing could be done to curb the destruction. It was later rebuilt and the banking competitors, who once faced each other from opposite sides of the street, ended up merging in 1993 into one joint bank, CB North. The current president of this bank, Mr. Francis Flanders, was instrumental in getting the revised edition of *Summer Resort Life* into print by providing the necessary funding and financial advice.

*　*　*

The late Lee Bisbee, who summered at the Belvedere Resort, shared a lively story about the early days of Charlevoix banking procedures, which was told to him by his father. The Indian fishing community, like everyone else, had to take out loans to finance their industry. They were reportedly not only frequently in debt, but behind on their payments to the two local banks in town, headed by Robert Bridge and Archie Livingston. Thus, whenever the bank examiners came to town, these friendly rivals, Bridge and Livingston, devised an ingenious way of shifting the debts back and forth between the two banks to avoid detection of the overdue debt by the bank examiners, and consequently the bankers never received reprimands for holding such risk paper.

These are the memories that make up the charm and the very essence of a small town. It behooves us to record and preserve our remaining landmarks — our parks, our shuffleboard courts, our fish ponds — so that everyone may enjoy these landmarks for generations to come.

BIBLIOGRAPHY:

The Traverse Region, H. R. Page & Co. Chicago, 1884.

Charlevoix — Vacation Glimpses, Earl D. Babst, 1944.

The Belvedere Club, Seeman & Peters Inc., 1969.

Pioneer Days of Charlevoix, by Mrs. Albert F. Bridge, 1923.

This Midwest Resort, John G. Rauch, Country Publishing Co., Inc.

Seventy Years of Sequanota History, Private Printing.

Bob Miles' Charlevoix, Charlevoix Historical Society, 1976.